Original stories by

**His Holiness The Dalai Lama, Paul McCartney,
Willie Nelson, Dennis Kucinich, Russell Simmons,
Brigitte Bardot, Martina Navratilova, Stella McCartney,
Ravi Shankar, Oliver Stone, Helen Thomas...**

and Dozens of Other Extraordinary Individuals

One Can Make a Difference

HOW SIMPLE ACTIONS CAN CHANGE THE WORLD

Ingrid E. Newkirk
with Jane Ratcliffe

Avon, Massachusetts

Whatever you can do or dream you can, begin it.

Boldness has genius, power and magic in it!

—John Anster in a loose interpretation of Goethe's *Faust*

Copyright © 2008 by Ingrid E. Newkirk
All rights reserved.
This book, or parts thereof, may not be reproduced in any
form without permission from the publisher; exceptions are
made for brief excerpts used in published reviews.

Published by
Adams Media, an F+W Publications Company
57 Littlefield Street, Avon, MA 02322. U.S.A.
www.adamsmedia.com

ISBN-10: 1-59869-629-7
ISBN-13: 978-1-59869-629-5

Printed in the United States of America.

J I H G F E D C B A

Library of Congress Cataloging-in-Publication Data
is available from the publisher.

The views expressed herein are those of each individual contributor and
not necessarily those of the authors or the publisher.

This publication is designed to provide accurate and authoritative information with regard to the subject matter covered. It is sold with the understanding that the publisher is not engaged in rendering legal, accounting, or other
professional advice. If legal advice or other expert assistance is required, the
services of a competent professional person should be sought.
    —From a *Declaration of Principles* jointly adopted by a Committee of the
American Bar Association and a Committee of Publishers and Associations

Many of the designations used by manufacturers and sellers to distinguish
their product are claimed as trademarks. Where those designations appear in
this book and Adams Media was aware of a trademark claim, the designations have been printed with initial capital letters.

The pages of this book are printed on 100% post-consumer recycled paper.

This book is available at quantity discounts for bulk purchases.
For information, please call 1-800-289-0963.

Acknowledgments

For their help in reaching busy people, thanks go to Marjorie Fields-Harris, Simone Reyes, Alexi Tavel, Ina Behrend, Suzie Gilbert, Mandi Warrren, Claudine Erlandson, Holly Dearden, Stephane Jasper, Annaig Lamoureux, Paul Margolin, Mia McDonald, Mandi Warren, Katie Annen, Betty Oyugi, P. Gay Harrah, Lavinia Browne, Brenda Young, Chhime R. Chhoekyapaa and Karla Waples; for her most valuable practical assistance, Starza Kolman with help from Sara Chenoweth, Laura Brown, and Philip Schein; for their patience, Tony LaRussa, Mickey Rourke, Peter Barss, Robert Thurman, Marc Bekoff, Olav Heyerdahl, Robin Janiszeufski-Hesson, Jennifer Lauck, Jonathan F. P. Rose, and Steph Davis; for much more than suggesting this book in the first place, Mary Ann Naples; for helping make the work come together at Adams Media, Beth Gissinger and Katrina Schroeder; and, of course, to the essayists, Barbara Adams, Sean Astin, Kevin Bacon, Brigitte Bardot, Dr. Neal Barnard, Carol Buckley, Lady Bunny, Sue Coe, Susan Cohn, The Dalai Lama, Pierre Dulaine, Dr. Armida Fernandez, Kathy Freston, Sharon Gannon, John Gardner, Andy Grannatelli, Temple Grandin, Peter Hammarstedt, Ru Hartwell, Larry Harvey, Dr. Henry Heimlich, Dana Hork, Rebecca Hosking, Robin Kevan, Representative Dennis Kucinich, Heidi Kuhn, Raymond Kurzweil, Bonnie-Jill Laflin, Wangari Maathai, Lily Mazahery, Sir Paul McCartney, Stella McCartney, Mark McGowan, Keith McHenry, John McLaughlin, Arthur Mintz, Moby, Aimee Mullins, Martina Navratilova, Willie Nelson, Petra Nemcova, Wade Rathke, Doris Richards, Rachel Rosenthal, Dave Seegar, Ravi Shankar, Reverend Al Sharpton, Russell Simmons, Anita Smith, Oliver Stone, Helen Thomas, Cheryl Ward-Kaiser, Robert Young, and Benjamin Zephaniah, all of whom have contributed to a better world.

Contents

Contents

Introduction

You cannot teach a man anything;
you can only help him find it within himself.

—Galileo (1564–1642, Italian astronomer and mathematician)

John O'Farrell, the English political writer and humorist, once noted how often people begin, "If I won the lottery, I would . . . ." Meaning that they would give more money to charity, feed the poor, go out and climb a mountain. He reminds us that, actually, we have won the lottery. That we scratched off our ticket on the day we were born and discovered that we were, say, a middle-class able-bodied person living in a Western country. (Rather than scratching it off, like most of the ticket holders, and finding we have been born a desperately poor child in a Third World slum or, God forbid, a despised cockroach.) He suggests that we count our blessings, our wealth, our health, our abilities. Count them a whole lot, and then set out to share them.

The wonderful thing is that the world is open to us, especially if we want to do positive things. We are surrounded by individuals, past and present, some stars, most not, who have followed their dreams, started programs, written books, invented useful gadgets, educated others, and simply turned what moves them into the magic of their lives. This book gathers the thoughts and insights of fifty such people whose sole wish is to help inspire similar changes in you.

Had Albert Schweitzer been alive, he would have been the first person on my list of essayists. I recently narrated an introduction to the remake of a 1957 documentary about this man who never wished to waste a moment of his life. Well into his eighties, he was tending to the sick in equatorial Africa, living in one room, working late into the evening, then playing his beloved organ music before going to sleep, satisfied with another day of service.

By and large, Dr. Schweitzer had a happy childhood (although he was teased by other boys at school for being overly serious), but it always troubled him that he had more than so many in the world. Cruelty upset him, and once, when he was asked to take up a slingshot and aim at birds who were happily singing their songs in the trees on the hillside, he sprang up and ran to shoo them away instead. From that moment on, he realized he could stop suffering. That is what motivated him to learn how to build a hospital in the jungle and to spend the time it took to get a medical degree so that he could serve in it. The phrase he coined, after much deliberation, was "Reverence for Life." He extended that reverence to all animals: cats, goats, and the pelicans he had treated for illness that were always the first to greet incoming human patients who traveled to his hospital by canoe.

Watching out for others, fighting for their right to be treated with dignity and respect no matter where they are from, what their language, how many legs or arms they have, or whether you know them personally, is a great way for us to share our riches. Helping others translates into helping ourselves. And the better we feel, the more delight and energy we have to channel into helping others. What a wonderful cycle of change and joy our lives can be!

As the president of the largest animal rights organization in the world, PETA, I have spent the last twenty-five years traveling constantly and attending everything from community workshops to corporate board meetings, speaking on college campuses and to legislators, meeting people from all walks of life, including the rich and poor, foreign dignitaries, Hollywood stars, and private citizens. My most cherished encounters are with people who have social concerns, caring people who want to contribute to a better world.

Surprisingly, whether I'm in Mumbai or Missouri, Manchester, England, or Manchester, New Hampshire, people ask me the same question, over and over again: "How can I, living here, doing what I do, possibly make any difference?" They'll say, "Oh, it's easy for you to make an impact. But I'm no one of importance. No one would listen to me." If I have learned anything, it is that they are wrong. Dead wrong. The world is waiting to hear from them, just as it is waiting to hear from you.

The first person to remind me of this was a nurse named Sue. Years ago, Sue was living with her mother and father in Delaware. One day, soon after PETA started but long before it became a household word, I received a letter from her. She wrote that she cared a great deal about animals and that the ways in which they are cruelly treated upset her. "But," she went on, "I feel helpless to have any impact. I've looked, but there is no group here for me to join. I am in the middle of nowhere."

I called Sue that evening. Sure enough, she was a deeply caring person who was willing to volunteer a few hours every week to help animals even if she had to drive many miles to do so. "Sue," I said. "If there's no group where you are, don't sit around waiting for someone else to start one. You must start one yourself." It took a little work to convince Sue that she could overcome her fear of public speaking and that like-minded souls would come out of the woodwork once things were rolling. The short version of the story is that Sue took a deep breath and did just that. Within a few months, her knowledge and her files grew like bamboo in a rainforest. After putting up notices on bulletin boards announcing her new group and after setting up a few literature tables at the local mall, she soon became the "go-to" person for local media calls and school talks on animal issues. Sue not only awakened and engaged a whole community, but she felt useful and fulfilled, finally doing what meant a great deal to her. Her life had new meaning, and, by extension, others' lives were slowly changed as well. What started with a small wish to contribute ended up nurturing a plant whose tendrils today reach into every junior high school from Wyoming to Winnipeg with materials Sue helped develop.

This example is about someone who wanted to help animals, but the crux of it pertains to anyone hoping to change the status quo. There are as many worthwhile ways to make a mark as there are people. Sue's worries simply reflect the ubiquitous "who am I?" question. Who am I to make a difference in a world in which huge corporations control the marketplace; massive empires run the media; the government turns a blind eye on the poor, the indigent, and the elderly; the environment is being laid to waste; animals are kept in chains to "entertain" us in circuses; children go uneducated and often uncared for; and excess food is discarded in one part of the world while millions starve in another?

Such discouraging observations can form a never-ending list, but they should be no deterrent! There is a saying I love that does away with that list of horrors. All you have to do is look at society's "impossibilities"—like, aptly enough, the collapse of the Berlin Wall—that became possible, sometimes overnight, and know this saying is as true as it is wonderful. It goes like this: "If you bang your head against a brick wall long enough, the wall will fall." And once you start banging your head against that wall, others will join you.

In this book, you will discover essays written by people who have harbored a variety of desires, faced the accompanying challenges, and been spurred into action, borne into action, or found themselves inching forward into a new role that now fits them beautifully. Each essayist—and I have chosen a deliberately diverse group spanning ages and interests—invites you to peek into his or her psyche. Fueled by enthusiasm (a feeling the ancient Greeks regarded as a holy state), optimism, and determination, and often armed with nothing grander than their own beliefs, each has pursued a course that beckoned to them. Through their essays we are permitted to see what was and is inside their hearts, to hear of their personal evolution, to learn what pitfalls and high points they found on the journey to helping themselves overcome a fear or problem, from which we can take a lesson, or in carving their name on society's rock. Some of these names will be familiar to you, others will not. By including both the "known" and the "unknown," I hope this book illustrates (a) that even those we admire from afar invariably face obstacles and have to find ways to keep their belief alive and (b) that you don't have to be a household name to make a difference, to become an example to others; you just need to have conviction. Hopefully, their stories will inspire you to find your own path, just as the influences I encountered in my youth inspired me to be true to myself.

I wasn't born fearless, but in no small part due to my father, who took great risks in his adventures, I soon became so. My father drove across the notorious sinking sands of the Indian desert known as the "Little Rani of Kutch," braved landslides and typhoons, took his small boat out at the first sign of a squall in the gulf, and climbed ice mountains in ordinary shoes! And while much of this was work related, he categorized it as pleasure. Under his tutelage, I grew to be fearsomely opinion-ated about anything that mattered to me, from the "right" way to spit cherry pits to how people treated their dogs. If I turned my vigor toward my family with some impassioned plea to not eat chicken or let me take up the piano instead of the violin, my weary mother would say, "Dear girl, I think you would argue with Jesus Christ himself if he walked into this room."

During my childhood, I was inspired by the adventurers who dared traverse the Sahara Desert on foot, though it was commonly accepted it couldn't be done. Or the brave Sher-pas who climbed Mount Everest in flimsy shoes and cotton trousers, without the benefit of supplemental oxygen. If they had listened to their insecurities, rather than to their powerful hearts, they would most likely have never left home. During this time, I also wanted to be a ballerina like Dame Margot Fonteyn or a great pianist like Chopin, but I had such poor balance I toppled our pyramid during the school gym class presentation for parents' day and I couldn't stretch my small fingers all the way to an octave and I'm almost tone deaf. I do believe, however, that if either of these had been my passion, the way moral values came to be, I would have applied myself with the diligence, desire, and fortitude that have helped me champion animals' rights.

When I was sixteen, I met a disciple of the great Indian poet Rabindranath Tagore, who rejected the material world in favor of service to others. I was moved by his profound con-nection to nature and his encouragement to share what you have with others, in particular the poor. Tagore became my hero. His words still rest upon my desk today:

I slept and dreamt that life was joy
I awoke and saw that life was service
I acted and behold, service was joy.

In my twenties, I was deeply inspired by Sojourner Truth. Sojourner was a black liberationist who stood up to white men who not only mocked her, but even tried to set fire to the buildings in which she spoke. When she was ridiculed for daring to address an assembly of "learned" men, she said, "If your jug holds a quart, and mine a pint, wouldn't you be mean not to let me have my half measure full?" Those words convinced me that everyone deserves a voice, even those who have none of their own and must let others speak for them. Her actions spurred me to gather five like-minded friends together to form PETA and so give the animals the voice they deserve.

Perhaps Sojourner Truth was born fearless, but more likely, she overcame her fears because her empathy for others and her loathing of injustice were so great. Courage can be found. One of the things my heroes taught me was that the present moment is extremely precious. Perhaps you will live a full and long life. Or perhaps you will only have a short time to leave a positive footprint. Either way, it's worth remembering the adage, "If at first you don't succeed, try and try again." Who cares if you don't do things exactly right the first time? Think of Robert the Bruce, sitting in a damp cave in Scotland, eons ago, believing he could never roust the English king from his lands. Deeply dejected, he sat watching a spider try and fail, once, twice, six times, to attach a thread to the cave wall so as to build her web. On the seventh try, she succeeded! Inspired by this tiny insect's tenacity, Bruce went back into the battle, determined to defeat the invaders. And win he did.

Everyone cares about something bigger than themselves, and everyone can make that cause a vital part of their lives no matter who they are. Someone "ordinary" was the first to step up to the plate and champion rights for blacks, for orphans, for people with disabilities, for animals, for women, for prisoners, and for humanity. Some of the most indispensable inventions and delightful distractions came about because someone, somewhere, dedicated countless hours to whatever interested or intrigued them, a problem of life and death perhaps, or tinkered about with, say, a musical instrument, a style or even something to eat. Think William Wilberforce, Robert Wilhelm Bunsen, Leo Fender, Johnny Appleseed, the Flying Wallenders, Florence Nightingale, Margaret Mead, Amelia Earhart, Lord Sandwich, Edward R. Murrow, George Washington Carver, Georgia O'Keefe, George Allen, and Mother Teresa. Their names live on for good reason. Perhaps yours will too.

I hope that this book brings you hope, courage, and inspiration, that it helps you examine your own ability to bash through those brick walls and encourages you to cast aside any doubts, hesitation, or perceived limitations you may be harboring. May it prove to you that you are bound by nothing at all and that the future, and your life, can be what you make it.

Head in the Stars, Feet on the Ground

Bobbie (Barbara) Adams earned her "fifteen minutes of fame" when she turned up for jury duty in Little Rock, Arkansas, dressed in her Star Fleet Commander uniform. The trial: Whitewater. Over the past decade, she has inspired thousands of people by stretching her fifteen minutes out into the galaxy. She has appeared in three documentaries about Star Trek and its followers; on National Public Radio and in newspapers internationally; and in Norway, where fans held a "BarbaraCon" convention in her honor. She still hears from people from all over the world who thank her for "being brave enough to be yourself." And although she just shakes her head and says that it had never occurred to her not to wear her uniform, "just as someone in the U.S. military might wear theirs," she is glad if her "small act of individuality" has inspired others to be true to themselves.

I am inspired by her total lack of hesitation in being true to herself. That quiet courage is reason enough for me to want to share her thoughts with you. And, should you think otherwise, Bobbie is far from the stereotype of an obsessed fan. She's not that interested in the actors who appear in Star Trek or the gossip and palaver surrounding the series. "I'm not pretending to be someone on a ship, not pretending to be in space. I'm just me." What interests her, and has since the show started (when she was two years old), are the Star Fleet's values and how people in this century can become mature enough to eventually embrace them. In an age where people's eyes seem to be melded into

1

their computer screens and we are more comfortable text messaging one another than conversing in person, Bobbie's sense of not only individuality, but also of community service, respect, inclusion, and reliability can serve as a worldwide template for our generation. You might say that she inspires us to go, if not where no man has gone before, to a place where we can happily be ourselves.

A lot of science fiction, certainly the first *Star Trek* series, allows us to look at what we are doing today as if from the future. This, in turn, allows us to be able to look more honestly at the progress we need to make to become truly civilized. This sort of distance provides a comfortable way to critique our times and our behaviors. I was too young to understand then, but I know now that during all the turmoil of the 1960s many people took comfort in the ideas that *Star Trek* put forth: that humans had managed not to sink and destroy each other, but to make it into the twenty-third century, that they had survived. That gave people hope. Not only that, right from the start there was total integration of sex, race, and species. It was a model of inclusion. No one questioned putting a female, a black female, on the bridge, for example, even back then. That appealed to me.

So did their practice of respect for others, no matter how different from us they might be. My parents were nonjudgmental and that's how I grew up. You made sure that you had all the facts, that you weren't reacting badly to someone or something without realizing that perhaps you didn't know everything you should. We were living in Brooklyn, where there was almost every possible ethnicity and culture; different foods, other languages you couldn't necessarily understand. On *Star Trek*, communication comes in all sorts of forms, too. Not every life form speaks the same language or has the same customs, but all must be respected. I remember being upset that my niece was often laughed at for how she looked. She had a big tumor on her nose, so the others laughed at her. But she couldn't help how she appeared, and it was several years before she could have surgery to remove the growth. I was also made fun of because I was, and still am, very short. This sort of disrespectful behavior has always seemed wrong to me.

The law within the United Federation of Planets is that you do not interfere with other cultures by trying to impose your own. You promote awareness of activities, but you do not force change upon others. In other words, lead by example. Know that humanity in the twenty-first century is like a little child that has yet to mature. The more we learn about others, about animals and humans and nature and science, the more we will evolve to be more understanding and inclusive. Laws that were written a century or two ago were relevant to their time, but times change and we improve. Another important thing *Star Trek* emphasized is taking responsibility. At this stage in our society's development, we still seem to find it easier to place blame, to sue someone if we trip over our own feet, for example. We have to learn not to place blame.

I am the fleet commander of our local Federation Alliance, and integral to our small group is community service. We dress in our uniforms and visit children in the local hospital, who get bug-eyed with delight when they see us walk in. We have raised money for the local animal shelter for about four years now. We have done a blood drive for the Red Cross, and we had an exhibit in the local Children's Museum with all the items donated from our members' own collections.

I hold two more principles close to my heart. First, I never want anyone to be ashamed of wearing the Star Fleet uniform. It stands for something good, and so it should be worn with pride. Second, I think people should express themselves, not someone else. I hear mothers say that they have to buy their teenagers the latest jacket or sneakers or Izod this and that so they can express themselves. I want to say, "How can you express yourself by wearing what everyone else is wearing, and by wearing a label that expresses the designer or the company that produced it?" It isn't what you can afford that matters, it's what's inside that counts. Be you; express yourself, not someone else. Don't throw away the chance!

On Being a Good Son

Sean Astin began his career as a child star when he appeared as Mikey in The Goonies *when he was just thirteen. He has since made his mark as an actor in fifty films and TV shows (including* 24 *and* Monk*) and is perhaps best known for his role as Samwise Gamgee in* The Lord of the Rings *trilogy. His famous mother, Patty Duke, also made her debut at thirteen, starring as Helen Keller in* The Miracle Worker*. Coming from a troubled and dysfunctional family, Patty was subject to fits of depression and even attempted suicides, all of which had a deep effect on Sean. Patty Duke felt a great sense of relief when she was finally diagnosed as bipolar, and today she works to help others with mental illness. Sean has made it his business to help in that area, too. In fact, his compassion for all, of any species and with any problems, combined with the experiences he had as a child, makes him a wonderful role model for his own three daughters. I am happy he would share his thoughts with readers of this book.*

grew up in what could be described as "Hollywood adjacent." My parents were famous, and in the center of the Hollywood machine, but somehow, living a block away from UCLA in Westwood, California, my brothers and I were insulated from much of the fast-lane activity of show business. My life felt very

Reprinted by special permission of the author.

normal with Little League, friends, and neighborhood holidays. I'm sure, like most people, the first visions I had of my future reflected whatever was happening around me: firefighter, police officer, janitor, and so on. I do remember in the fourth grade, my mother told me that I could be anything I wanted to be, even president of the United States. This was a blessing and a curse, because for most of my life after that, I took her literally. While becoming president of the United States doesn't seem likely for me, even at thirty-six years of age, I remain convinced that I could be almost anything I want to be in life.

When I travel around the country, people often approach me about how much my mother has meant to them and how grateful they are that she's spoken openly about her bipolar mood disorder. I'm always moved by these conversations. Obviously, her condition had a major impact on our family. I spent a great deal of time worrying about her and wishing that I had the tools to ease her suffering. Out of a feeling of gratitude to the hardworking mental health care professionals who helped my mom, I felt duty-bound to contribute to our national public conversation about mental health by sharing openly about our life. I've also been invited by a major pharmaceutical company to participate in a bipolar awareness campaign. And I've launched a Web site where we provide a mood questionnaire to help folks determine if they or a loved one may have symptoms of the disease as well as supplying tools and resources so that people can find the assistance they need.

I've also been involved in advocating for a host of issues, problems, and areas of concern in our society. Oftentimes, celebrities, notables, activists, and others focus most of their attention on one or two specific issues that mean the most to them, or that they can have the greatest impact on. Unfortunately, I never developed the skill to filter, prioritize, compartmentalize, or ignore my feelings about anything that bothers me in the world. It may be arrogance or a melodramatic fantasy of how the universe should operate, but I can't help feeling as though not only can I make a difference in the world, but that if I don't, I will have failed to honor my own destiny. The one thought that gets me off my duff is that no one person can improve everything alone. And there's no chance that everything will improve unless everyone does something.

One of my proudest endeavors in the civic realm relates to the issue of literacy. In particular, the family literacy movement. I'm a spokesperson for the National Center for Family Literacy as well as a Verizon Literacy Champion. Recently, my wife and I founded a literacy success award given to individuals who've used their newfound literacy to overcome obstacles and move on to healthier, happier lives that benefit others. I've never been diagnosed with ADD, dyslexia, or any type of learning disability, but I know for certain that in grade school, I had neither the patience nor discipline to complete my assignments. One of my most cherished memories is of the period of time when my mother would read entire books aloud to me. The words, concepts, and rhythms in the stories have not only stayed with me, but they have been my weapons to do battle with the world. My father always overemphasized the critical importance of academia. The combination of my mother's and father's values operating on me had the effect of inspiring in my soul an intense and passionate devotion to literacy. In my heart, I believe that people's ability to read and think—in essence, to communicate—is the last best hope that mankind has for peace in the world.

My father presented me with a copy of Rudyard Kipling's great poem "If" at the surprise twenty-fifth birthday party my

wife threw for me. I reread it many times every year. Everything you need to know about how to behave in life is in it;
keeping your head about you in times of crisis, letting yourself
dream, never dealing in lies, and, remembering the power and
worth of virtue.

Saving the World by Degrees

An extremely talented actor (among his screen credits: JFK, Animal House, Diner, Footloose, A Few Good Men, *and on stage:* Lemon Sky *and* Spike Heels*), Kevin is a family man who cares about the planet and all the beings on it. He has won critical acclaim for giving so much of himself in his acting, but the reason he belongs in this book is that he is also giving in other ways.*

The phenomenally popular game Six Degrees of Kevin Bacon *was invented by students at Albright College in Pennsylvania in 1994. It requires players to try to connect any film actor in history to Kevin Bacon as quickly as possible with as few links as possible. Elvis Presley has a "Bacon number" of two (Elvis appeared in* Change of Habit *with Ed Asner and Ed Asner was in* JFK *with Kevin Bacon). If you are not an actor, hey, you are probably still connected to Kevin, at least as a member of an audience. That's because he has appeared in so many different roles in various media that possibly only a few tribal people still living without benefit of a satellite dish somewhere haven't seen him in something. I myself have a photograph of Kevin standing next to me at PETA's "Rock against Fur" concert in New York. I'm proud to say that gives me a Bacon number of one.*

Kevin has put his notoriety to good use. SixDegrees.org is the celebrity-driven Web site he founded (Joaquin Phoenix, Tyra Banks, and Bette Midler, among others, advertise their favorite causes on the site) to encourage charitable giving. It is also a game: anyone can enter his or her favorite charity, and there are even "races" that net extra funds for the most popular of visitors' causes. Given the need in the world, Kevin has done something wonderful by coming up with a game in which everyone wins.

Acting is a very self-involved line of work. I've been act-ing since before I knew what it was. I remember one of my first toys, when I was very little, was a costume box that my mother had filled with old clothes. Basically, I had a strong desire to be watched, to have people look at me, so I would dress up and become different characters. Most actors tend not to like to admit that they just want to be noticed, but that's what it is.

However, no matter how much you want to put yourself out there, no matter how much you want the attention, doing so can be frightening. Over the years, I've learned that fear is an important emotion, that if we harness it properly it can drive us and push us toward new challenges. For example, my band, the Bacon Brothers, played Carnegie Hall in 2007, just one song: a tribute to Bruce Springsteen. Bruce is a huge hero to me, so it was very frightening to think I had to stand up and try to interpret one of the Master's works, especially because we were doing it very differently, with an accordion, a cello, and we changed up the guitar. I was sitting in the dressing room, stressing out and Bruce walked in. It was a heart in my mouth kind of moment but it probably made me play better!

The same is true with the stage. Everything can go wrong on stage: it's live and so there's always danger. A prop falls, you forget your lines, someone in the front row starts snoring, a cell phone goes off. I get butterflies in my stomach, at times my knees have actually been shaking, I've been nauseous and short of breath, but luckily I don't sweat a lot! That kind of fear keeps you on your toes, makes you work harder. With movies, it's a different fear because a movie set is comfortable to me; it's like my living room. But even then, things can go wrong with a stunt or something, and there's still always the fear that the movie will come out and no one will see it or—maybe this is worse—if they do, they'll discover what a big fraud you are! Another good thing about fear is the tremendous rush that comes when it's over. The feeling that you've conquered. Perhaps for that reason, I love amusement rides, but I don't jump out of planes. That's too much of a good thing!

In my personal life, I worried that I wasn't doing enough for the world. It can be hard to figure out what to do. Celebrities are asked constantly to go to benefits. You could do a benefit a night and so it's hard not to get too spread out. I'm devoted to my family, my wife, but I also want to help. You know how you feel when you pick up the newspaper in the morning and read about the bodies, people and animals dying, hunger, climate change? It can be overwhelming. I'm raising two kids and I see that sense of hopelessness sometimes present with their generation. I want to reach out and do something about that. People like Bono are doing great campaigns in Africa, Live Aid; other people have found ways to help. I was thinking about it all one day while I was putting some of Paul Newman's dressing on my salad. I realized that Paul raised hundreds of millions of dollars for good causes just by doing what he likes to do, cooking. I thought "what brands me?" and that gave me an idea.

I'll admit that when I first heard about *Six Degrees of Kevin Bacon* I didn't like it. I thought it was a joke at my expense. I think that's part of the fear thing, your head gives in to that and you think people are laughing at you. But, as time went on, I met the guys that conceived the idea and I realized that they had a real fondness for my work. They had chosen me because of the sheer number of films I have crammed into my life. I've taken the little and the big parts and I've been in films in which I was one of a huge cast—every actor in the world was in *JFK*. That made me the ideal "six degrees" guy. It was cool! I thought, "That's my brand now. I can use that." Because I do believe that we're all connected, not just in movies or photographs, but in the world. All of us crawled out of the same swamp. Nothing happens in a vacuum, the butterfly flaps her wings in one part of the world and there's an effect in another; we use all this fuel in the West and there's severe flooding thousands of miles away across the ocean. The idea comes up all the time now. I bought the domain name, *www.sixdegrees.org*, brainstormed with friends and family, and the folks at Network for Good who said, "Great, we'll do it with you" and created a new way to give.

Through this site, people can learn about and support various charities. It's celebrity-driven, which gives us press attention for the causes. But anyone can put up a badge for their favorite charity. You can say, "I believe in animal rights," "I want to find a cure for autism," or whatever moves you. We have little races to see which charity gets the most donations and then I donate my own money to boost the top ones. I'm excited because it's a viral sort of thing. People like to go to Amazon.com to shop and online charity giving is as easy as that. I'm hoping it spreads exponentially. People get in touch with each other this way. They can post pictures of their friends, say "this is my favorite band," and "by the way, let's help save the rainforest." That's powerful stuff. That's the kind of "six degrees" we need to tap into.

Doing good work makes you feel good, makes you feel as if you have some control over your life and your future. I have this joke motto: someone asks me, "How are you doing?" and my answer is "I'm doing what I can with what I've got." That can work for everyone.

Sex Kitten and Matriarch of Mice

Brigitte Bardot's movies were the talk of the Western world. She made fifty of them in twenty years, some light French farces, some sex romps on the beach, perhaps none more well known than Et Dieu Crea Eve, *or* And God Created Woman. *She was the epitome of the fantasy female. She was, however, deeply unhappy in the role. And, although she stuck it out for twenty years, she did it while fighting depression. At the age of forty, Brigitte Bardot took her pouty lips and went home to the south of France, vowing never to appear on the screen again. She had made the decision to do what her heart told her she must: champion the cause of animal rights. No matter what directors said or did to try to persuade her to return—and many tried hard to get her back—when Madam Bardot said "non!" she meant "non!"*

In 2006, I happened to go to Paris to protest Jean-Paul Gautier's use of baby foxes as panels in a frock coat (the bodice of which was made of calves' hide trimmed with lamb). Madam Bardot had been in the city a few days before, on the occasion of the twentieth anniversary of the Brigitte Bardot Foundation, and had delivered a rousing speech to thunderous applause about the responsibility to stop cruelty. Now, from her home outside St. Tropez, she heard on the nightly news that I had been arrested. She immediately fired off a letter to the jail and, more importantly, to Monsieur Gautier, asking him to be decent enough to hear the animals' cries and creative enough to abandon fur designs. As soon as I heard of her action, I was reminded that her sassiness, her independence, and her activism belonged in this book.

had an unhappy childhood, but I have a happy childhood memory. When I was ten years old, I managed to rescue a tiny mouse who appeared at our dinner table. My father wanted to kill this little creature, but, luckily, she ran up my sleeve into my sweater. My parents thought that I was itching, that I had a rash. It was quite funny! Later on, during the night, I went downstairs and released her into our garden. I saved her! It was my first official animal rescue and one of the most fulfilling moments of my life, although I wasn't aware of it at the time.

My career in film was busy and exotic, but it was never very fulfilling. Of course, I have lots of memories of those times, but, honestly, they're more of a nuisance than anything else! I was often depressed by that way of life. Sometimes I couldn't really overcome my sadness during these cinema days. I couldn't imagine myself in such a world forever, and on occasion I wanted to simply stop living. I even attempted suicide, but, fortunately, I didn't succeed. I stayed in the business because I told myself, and my mother told me, that I needed money. I didn't have a dime, I was just a kid. I thought that I needed money to be able someday to protect animals. I had an affinity for all of them, little birds kept in cages so that they cannot stretch their wings and fly, rabbits who are killed to be eaten. This thought of how to help them began to consume my life.

When I was eighteen, I married the great French director, Roger Vadim, and we started making movies together. It was Vadim who told me about vivisection, animal experiments. That absolutely chilled and haunted me. He told me of how animals suffer in laboratories, in their cages. I found it shocking that humans could be so horribly cruel. This passion for animals carried over into movies. I loved the little animals in my films so much that I couldn't let them go and would keep them. I had a very small apartment in Paris, and one day I rescued a performing monkey from a production and took him home. He broke everything in the place, he ate all my makeup, and he soiled everywhere. I was very young then, about nineteen years old, and I became upset, even angry, but I felt sorry for him, too. I knew that he couldn't help it. I finally took him to a sanctuary for exotic animals where he was very happy.

All my life I've been touched by particular cases that I didn't understand fully but that I could feel so deeply. Stories about slaughterhouses shocked me even when I was small, but, as horrible as it made me feel, I didn't know what to do about it. Then, in 1986, I sold everything that had a monetary value to start my foundation for animals. People ask if that was a difficult thing to do. No, not at all! Well, it was a little hard to find myself selling the very first diamond that I bought myself! It was difficult because my mother had told me to buy it and I remember the moment well. I must have been twenty-three or twenty-four years old. She warned me that it was best not to keep money but buy precious stones instead. She said if there is a war, if there are social problems, at least with a diamond, you can hide it on yourself, in your panties, and you can always survive with a precious stone!

So, we went to Mellerio's—a large French jewelry store, the equivalent of Cartier. I don't know if it's still there, in the fabulous Place Vendome in Paris. I paid for this diamond with my very first large fees from my films. When I sold it to support the work of the Brigitte Bardot Foundation for Animals, I felt quite sentimental. I never wore that ring, it wasn't for wearing, but it was symbolic! But there it was on the auction block, and I knew I was getting much better use out of it than having it sit in a vault in a bank.

When I see people eating animals, I always say "Animals are my friends, and I don't eat my friends." But I never forbid anyone to eat meat. I just wish that they would eat less if they're not going to be vegetarians. When I was a kid, we ate meat once a week. We ate fish, eggs, and pasta, and we didn't put meat on the pasta. We had meat only on Sundays, once a week. No one needs to eat meat morning, noon, and night. It's very bad for your health and it's really a horror for the animals, a dreadful industrial death, with conditions getting worse.

I quit the cinema thirty-three years ago, and since then I have had no help whatsoever in my animal protection work from the French government. None! However, I have had help from foreign countries. It is scandalous and sad. I must have seen fifty ministers, three presidents of the Republique, I forget how many representatives, yet the French government has never helped. They would do well to listen to the words of Leo Tolstoy, words that I believe in. He said, "As long as there are slaughterhouses, there will be battlefields." It's formidable and apropos in these frightening times, when we see more and more battlefields and more and more slaughterhouses opening up all over the world.

There's no relief at all for these poor animals that go to the slaughter. It's abominable. I think animals help us live; they've helped me live. It was only when I began to devote myself to protecting animals that I blossomed completely. Taking care of them, looking out for them, has given my life true meaning, a meaning I hope future generations can also experience. Young people are always a hope. More of them must realize that the animal is not an object for profit, not a toy for our amusement, hunted for sport, not some thing to be cut up for his fur. They may see that the animal has the right to live, just as we have the right to live. We, the animals, the plants are the whole, and the whole makes a chain, and if we break that chain, all of humanity will pay. That's it.

These days, I have horses, ponies, donkeys, goats, sheep, chickens, geese, cats, dogs, ducks, and, like George Clooney, I have four domestic pigs. Wild boars come on my property in the south of France and have their young. I have doves and lots of pigeons. And guess what? I have mice! And I don't want them killed! Even my cats respect them because they understand from me that the mice behind my little desk must not be touched. They are *musaraignes* (like shrews, field mice), very small with very pointed noses. No bigger than my thumb.... The dogs don't hurt them either because they've been asked to leave them alone, please! When the mice come to eat, I give them little crumbs and pieces of this and that and nobody moves! It's quite extraordinary because they aren't tame. They came to live in my bedroom behind my little desk and believe me, they're happy there because nobody touches my mice! Yes, the first one I saved was when I was ten years old, and here I am, saving mice again!

For me it is a vocation. I live only for them twenty-four hours a day, because if I didn't have them, I would have killed myself a long time ago. That's the truth. When you love, you devote yourself, body and soul, for the love you have for something; it can be religion, it can be for older people, children, perhaps world hunger, or whatever, but one must do it completely, one cannot do it halfway. That's why I left everything behind to be completely available to try to protect animals anywhere in the world ... because cruelty doesn't only occur in France; it's everywhere and with all animals.

Kisses to all who care.

A Healthy Outlook

Dr. Neal Barnard fits the description of an ethical physician as perfectly as a surgical glove fits the hand. I met him in the mid-1980s, when a scandal was erupting over the U.S. military's plan to suspend dogs in slings, shoot them, have medics practice emergency wound treatments on them, and then dispatch them. Dr. Barnard offered to help research alternatives, and thanks to him, the Department of Defense suddenly found 900 emergency-room physicians knocking on their door, eager to offer their services to train the young military medics without the use of animals. That helped win the case, and I will always be grateful to him.

An insightful, caring person and mentor to up-and-coming physicians, Dr. Barnard gave up his individual practice to devote himself fully to the charity he founded, the Physicians Committee for Responsible Medicine. He is a prolific author of books on the power of nutrition to prevent and combat disease, including Food for Life; Eat Right, Live Longer; Foods That Fight Pain; *and* Dr. Neal Barnard's Program for Reversing Diabetes. *His journey shows that setting your mind to a problem can help fix it!*

We didn't talk health food in North Dakota in the 1950s, especially those of us with families in the cattle business. My grandfather, uncles, and cousins all raised cattle, and roast beef, baked potatoes, and corn were our everyday fare. Except for special occasions, that is, when we ate roast beef, baked potatoes, and peas.

My father didn't care for the cattle business, and left it to go to medical school. Toward the end of college, I decided to do the same, and, while my medical school applications incubated, I took a job in the bowels of Fairview Hospital in Minneapolis. Located in an otherwise unused basement hallway, the hospital morgue was a desolate museum of medical tragedies. No living person ever went there if they didn't have to. The telephone was a hefty brick-like device from the 1940s, and the place suffered from general neglect. My job was to assist the pathologists as they examined the bodies. One day, a man died in the hospital of a massive heart attack (probably from eating hospital food, but that's another story). To expose the heart, we removed a section of ribs from his chest—an indelicate procedure performed with a hefty garden clipper—and we set the large pie-wedge of ribs next to the body. The pathologist knew I was headed for medical school, so he made sure to drill the details of each examination into my head. Slicing into a coronary artery, he pointed out the atherosclerotic plaque that had choked off the blood supply to the heart. And he found more plaques in the arteries to the brain, the kidneys, and the legs. He explained that these came from the cheeseburgers and steak Americans use as staples, something I hadn't heard before. At the end of the examination, I carefully put the ribs back in the chest, cleaned up the body, and went to the cafeteria to see what was for lunch. As it turned out, the day's featured dish was ribs. Between the look and the smell, eating them was not an option. I didn't become a vegetarian on the spot, but that was the day meat began to lose its appeal.

All to the good, because, although I was unaware of it at the time, research studies had already begun to indict the foods my family raised for their contribution to heart disease, diabetes, obesity, and hypertension, and to roughly half of all cancer cases. In fact, Western diets, centered on meats and dairy products, have a more negative effect on health than any other single factor. Like me, American medicine paid little attention to any of this. When I finished my medical training, I took a job at St. Vincent's Hospital in downtown New York. As I talked with my colleagues, I began to realize that we were good at diagnosis and reasonably good at treatment, but we were absolutely abysmal at prevention. We did nothing about heart attacks until they came through the emergency room doors. We did nothing about cancer until it showed up on a mammogram or blood test. Our collective task, as we saw it, was to clean up the wreckage of bad habits, bad genes, or bad luck. All the while, we neglected the most critical part of what doctors ought to be doing, and I resolved to change that.

In 1985, I started an organization called the Physicians Committee for Responsible Medicine (PCRM) in order to bring prevention and nutrition front and center in medical practice. The original plan was to build a group of perhaps fifteen or twenty doctors who would opine on these issues, and I began to advertise for like-minded physicians. But this mission touched a nerve, and more and more doctors began to join. Today more than 6,000 doctors belong to PCRM. We conduct research studies, focusing on the power of healthier diets. While we do not discount the value of drugs, we would like to see the roles of "conventional" medicine (i.e., medications) and "alternative" medicine (i.e., diet changes) reversed.

Often, a diet change is more powerful than drugs. In 2003, my research team began a study testing a new dietary approach to diabetes for the National Institutes of Health. We eliminated meat, dairy products, and other fatty foods, and emphasized fruits, vegetables, beans, and whole grains, and we compared this diet against a more traditional diabetes diet. A man named Vance read about the study and came in to see me. He described how his grandfather had died at age thirty, and how he was just thirty-one when he was diagnosed with diabetes. His weight had climbed over the years, and despite medication, his blood sugar was terribly out of control. We sat down and looked at how a low-fat vegan diet might help. He was glad that this was not just another pharmaceutical study. And, a bit to his surprise, he took to oatmeal, topped with apples and cinnamon, along with toast and fresh fruit. Lunch or dinner would be salads, dressed up with beans, blood oranges, or other additions. He enjoyed burritos, pasta, fresh vegetables, and fruits. As the weeks went by, his weight plummeted. After a year, he had lost sixty pounds. His blood sugar fell, too, to the point that he no longer needed medication. By rearranging his plate, he had tackled his disease. I was as thrilled as he was. Following a similar diet, I'm pleased to say that others have reversed heart disease, cured migraines, and relieved arthritis.

Now, some patients are a bit of a tough sell, as I learned from my own mother. My father and she still live in North Dakota, and she's had a high cholesterol level for years. Despite the fact that I'd done a number of studies on diet and health and had written several nutrition books, she wasn't interested in a diet overhaul. What finally put her over the edge was her own physician, who wanted to put her on cholesterol-lowering medications. For a woman born in 1924, the idea of being dependent on medication was simply out of the question. At that point, she picked up my book *Food for Life*, and started a vegan diet.

After six or seven weeks, she went back to her doctor for a cholesterol test. And to this day, she describes how he walked into the exam room, cholesterol report in hand, and began to apologize. Apparently, the laboratory equipment must be broken, he explained, because her cholesterol had seemingly plunged to normal levels—something that was clearly impossible in such a short time.

"But if this really were my cholesterol level, would I need medicine?" Mom asked.

"No," the doctor said. "That's my point. This is a totally normal cholesterol level. It can't be right."

My mother thanked him and left, drug free.

When I set up PCRM, I aimed to do more than conduct research studies. We also advocate for more ethical research. When we began, there had been several recent examples of blatantly unethical research practices, some involving humans, others involving animals. And our doctors spoke up about it. In a government experiment, short children were to be injected with a genetically engineered growth hormone to see if it would make them taller. The experiment would have been ethical had the children been deficient in growth hormone, but they were normal, healthy children, whose parents might have been a bit shorter than others. Evidence suggested that the hormone injections would increase cancer risk over the long run and pose other risks. I was horrified to discover that at the other end of the height spectrum, some doctors used massive estrogen doses to try to halt growth in tall girls. As they put it, a tall girl would have trouble finding a husband or getting a job as an airline stewardess, believe it or not, and estrogens could shut down their bone growth. Never mind that they increase the risk of cancer and infertility in the process.

Our doctors were also concerned about animal experiments. We remembered all too clearly our own experiences in "dog lab"—a ritual in which first- or second-year medical students are told to experiment on live dogs and ultimately kill them. The exercise is intended to convey the fine points of physiology, but ends up horrifying many students and desensitizing the rest. I had come to feel that typical animal research included much of the same callousness and inattention to other methods. There must be a way for science to move forward without blood on our hands. We worked with Harvard University to develop a method of teaching medical students by bringing them into the human operating room, where the drugs that had been used in "dog lab" were used in a more appropriate setting and where their effects could instantly be seen on the OR monitors. Today, nearly all U.S. medical schools have abandoned "dog labs."

While our work is nowhere near done, the problems—and their solutions—are clearer than ever. We need to break from the nutritional habits that I grew up with and that my family promoted. We need to break with the indifference that allows people to fall victim to illness, on the assumption that picking up the pieces is the most we can do. Most of all, we need to take suffering seriously—wherever it manifests and whomever it affects, and do what we can to heal it.

When I graduated from medical school, I took the Hippocratic oath. The classic Greek physician's most important admonition was "First, do no harm." I chose that as PCRM's motto, and consider it an important jumping off point for the decisions of everyday life.

When Life Gives You Elephants, Make Orange Juice

In the woods of Tennessee, there is a sanctuary for elephants lucky enough to have escaped forever from the hard life of the circus or the boredom of the zoo. You can watch them on a Webcam as they bathe in the lake, stroll up the hills, entwine their trunks in greeting, and play with the dogs (see the Resources section for the Web address). You might even see them making orange juice, but I'll let Carol Buckley explain that.

The Elephant Sanctuary, which Carol cofounded in 1995, means a lot to me. Growing up in India, I not only saw elephants in servitude—the howdah on their backs, the ankus or bull hook being dug into their sensitive flesh (yes, elephants can feel a fly land on their skin!)—but I also befriended a mahout, an elephant trainer. He told me the tragic story of how an elephant is "broken," separated from her mother and sisters and aunts, and how she pines for freedom and family her whole life long. Elephants are complex, social, intelligent beings, and Carol Buckley could hardly have picked a bigger project. Her ambition, her resolve, and her dream are perfect for this book.

I can remember the very first time I saw an elephant. They were on a little island at the zoo, and what didn't occur to me until later was that everywhere they turned, there were people staring at them. When I attended college, I took this amazing

"Semester at Sea" program where we sailed around the world. When we reached Africa, we went on a safari, and that's when I saw elephants again, only in their real home this time, in lush vegetation. I was struck by how this whole family of elephants was so calm. Along we came, a busload of screaming American girls, and the elephant families didn't pay any mind. They constantly touched each other with their trunks.

During my first year at college, I decided to work with animals. I began working with dogs and found I had a knack. One day I met someone who suggested that I learn to be a professional animal trainer. He gave me a pass to get behind the scenes at an animal park and apprentice with the trainers on staff. Thanks to his recommendation I was later accepted as a student at Moorpark College's Exotic Animal Training and Management Program, which, back then, was focused on training animals for circuses and zoos. Luckily, around that time, I met and became mesmerized by a baby elephant named Fluffie, who was used to draw customers to a tire store! Fluffie was only one year old and had just been imported. In fact, she was the second to last elephant to be imported into California before the Endangered Species Act became law and animal imports were banned. The tire store owner, Bob, let me volunteer to help with Fluffie's care. She was living in a truck at the tire store, but I lived on a half acre of land and managed to persuade Bob to let me take her home. That meant I had full control of her even on weekends, when she appeared at the tire store to "perform."

Fluffie, who I renamed Tarra, was very needy, and I quickly became overprotective of her. She was incredibly smart and very receptive. She loved learning games; everything interested her, and I had to find ways to challenge her continually. She enjoyed playing the xylophone and the harmonica, and would waltz and sit down. I didn't control her, I used simple requests that she understood, like "come" and "walk" and "sit." I would ask her to do things, and if she felt like it, she did. If she didn't, she didn't. With Tarra, it was a matter of patience, bananas, and waiting for her to do things in her time. Somehow the circus industry got wind of the fact that I was training this baby elephant. A man named Smoky Jones turned up. He offered his services to train Tarra "properly." He told me that if I carried on being too affectionate to Tarra, she would get aggressive, that if I loved her, I must discipline her. He said she would be brutalized and even end up dead, killed, if I didn't listen to him and make her obey. I refused to hand her over! Tarra's owner decided to hire Smoky Jones to train his elephant and me at his premises in Fontana, California. So off we went, Tarra and I, with a few of our belongings packed up in her tiny delivery truck, for four weeks under Smokey's tutelage. This was initiation into the world of performing elephants.

One year later, I had secured a contract for Tarra to perform at a theme park. When I got my paycheck, I divided it into two, paying half of all the expenses, including Tarra's truck repair and fuel, her food, and so on. That made me a partner in her care, so when Tarra's owner came to take her back one day, I was able to get a restraining order preventing her return. He was livid! "Buy her then," I was told! "For $25,000!" The going rate for an elephant then was $5,000–$7,000, but he was firm! I wasn't sure how I would cope, but I also believe that the Universe never gives you more than you need and never gives you more than you can deal with. My parents had faith in me. My father cosigned a loan, and Tarra became mine forever. All I had to do was stay on track.

I knew Tarra was growing up and needed a proper place to live. Also, as she grew up she began to show signs of restlessness. She was distracted and not interested in performing. I looked around but couldn't find anyplace where Tarra would be able to be herself, would be respected for who she is. The idea of starting a sanctuary started to prey on my mind. While I figured out how that dream could come true, I found a Canadian zoo where she could be with seven other elephants, and I was offered the job of superintendent of elephants. So we went there together, but it wasn't ideal for her; the sight of other elephants frightened her, and she spent all of her time at the gate, bobbing, a clear indication that she wanted out.

Over the next few years, Tarra and I moved to several different zoos, trying to find a place that met her needs. Finally recognizing that what I was looking for did not yet exist, my partner and I decided to purchase land and create a sanctuary especially for elephants. In 1994, when I heard that Tyke, a performing elephant, was gunned down in the street in Honolulu after running amok and killing her trainer, we knew the time was now. We found a piece of land. It was one hundred and twelve acres, which meant a $130,000 loan. I used some property I owned in California as collateral, and many people who knew Tarra came forward to help. It just started to all come together. Within three years, the Elephant Sanctuary had 15,000 dues-paying members. Up went our barns, we fenced more land, and every year we expanded, buying more and more acreage for the elephants to roam on.

On March 3, 1995, Tarra set foot on the sanctuary land. Next came our first rescued elephant, Barbara. She was a circus elephant who had been rejected by Ringling Brothers Barnum and Bailey, but was probably the wisest creature I've ever met. She was very knowing, clear about everything, and a great communicator. The minute she arrived, she was a teacher, bringing us closer to understanding the true nature of elephants. One unusual thing about Barbara was she used to make orange juice. She didn't like to eat oranges but loved juice. We'd put down her produce and she'd separate out all the oranges, leave them, and eat everything else. Then she would pull the oranges in, one by one, then squish them with her foot, completely, juicing them, keep the juice in one place, toss the peel away, and then suck the juice up with her trunk!

Next came Shirley and Jenny. Then Bunny, who had lived alone in a zoo for her entire life. For forty-four years, she had stood in the small flat dirt yard of her zoo enclosure. Her muscles never developed to navigate hills; she didn't know how to walk on anything uneven. Even a little dip in the ground would throw her. She couldn't figure out how to step down or up. One day, walking along a shallow creek edge at the sanctuary, she lost her footing and froze in shock, letting her body fall to the ground. I tried to calm her, reassure her, but she was frozen with fear. Then I looked up, and several hundred yards away, I saw Barbara standing in the barn doorway, watching. I returned to reassuring Bunny, trying to get her to relax, when, the next thing I knew, Barbara was crossing the creek. She calmly approached, touching Bunny all over her face and head, gently, with her trunk, then made a little rumble sound and walked away slowly. Bunny got up and followed her. That was Barbara, forever helping the other elephants. She lived only five years.

Barbara died so peacefully. She came into the barn during the day, which was unusual because it was a sunny day. I left the office and spent the day pampering her; it was my birthday and I wanted to celebrate it with her, scrubbing her, giving her a warm bath, trimming her nails, loving her. She'd just melt into it, she loved the affection. In hindsight, it was like a preparation for her passing. At five o'clock, her feeding time, she ate her mineral ball with goodies, her peanut and molasses ball, her supplements, and then, quite suddenly, she was on her side on the barn floor. We all knew she had a wasting disease. Before, if she could not stand, she would show that she wanted to get up, and we'd help push her up and then hoist her up with a harness built specifically for her. This time, she acted differently; she resisted our help. So we stopped. My eyes met hers, and I got it. She was telling us that she was dying and wanted us to let her go. I heard this from her as if in a voice. Three of us, Joanna, Scott, and I, were with her with our hands on her, and in fifteen minutes her breathing slowed. There was no struggle, no fighting for breath; she just went totally peacefully.

Tarra loved the sanctuary too. With her, freedom wasn't new. Even as we traveled together before the sanctuary existed, I would stop every day when on the road, somewhere interesting, let her out of her trailer so she could walk around, perhaps playing in a creek, river, or field. She was like a dog in that way, and we were best friends. Now, at the sanctuary we have eighteen elephants. They have come from all over: fifteen are Asian, three are African. Some of the needy elephants that come here are overwhelmed at first, shocked by the idea that they are free. They are incredibly pleased and they all eventually become quite accustomed to it. After all, that's how it should be.

There is a Persian proverb, "With kindness and a smile you can lead an elephant by a thread." This is the founding principle that guides us at the Elephant Sanctuary: respect the elephants and they will do their best to respect you.

I Just Want to Be Me

Lady Bunny has a wicked sense of humor and lives a "wicked" life, as she'll point out below. "She" is also built like a Mack truck, standing nearly seven feet tall in her skyscraper heels and bouffant updo. With legs so long they should be insured (Bunny claims she tones them by raising them over her head whenever possible), it is hard, as with a Scotsman's kilt, to resist the thought of taking a look up that micro-mini skirt to see how on earth she has so successfully hidden "her" various bits and bobs. The drag queen founder of Wigstock—New York's festival of drag—is quite a sight!

I first met Bunny (Jon Ingle behind all the pancake makeup), or The Bunion as she calls herself, at a PETA event. When one of the Humanitarian of the Year awardees graciously thanked his wife from the podium and the spotlight scanned the audience for a glimpse of this wonderful other half, Bunny leapt to her feet to take the bow as if she were the honoree's wife. Paul McCartney, who was in the audience, howled with laughter! Later, I went to her "Taste of Bunny" show at the Fez in New York and found myself grinning from the moment her introductory "credits" were announced: thanks for makeup to Sherwin Williams, body by Crunch (Nestlé's Crunch), and hair by Weed Eater. Over the years, I've learned that Bunny is always willing to help anyone who needs help, and not just with a quickie in the stairwell. She adds a unique contribution to this book because she has used her talents and chutzpah to challenge sexual stereotypes in the least serious ways imaginable: to have transexuality and homosexuality seen as something to celebrate rather than scorn.

Why did I become a drag queen, you ask? I say, well, honey, I don't know exactly, but I was sketching Marlo Thomas's flip from *That Girl* before I was six years old, as well as demanding dolls from my nervous religious parents. Years later, they confessed that they were worried that giving me dolls might make me gay. I told them, "If I was asking for them, I was already gay!" I've always identified with feminine things, even before I wore them myself. As a child, I wore my hair long and was sometimes confused for a girl. At ten or eleven, one Halloween I dressed as "a woman" with my best friend, Paul, as "my husband." With each doorway that I darkened, the fact that I wore a dress, some of mom's heels and a (totally tragic and frumpy) women's wig confirmed many of my neighbors' suspicions about my budding sexuality. Later, as was the fashion in the New Wave era, I wore makeup, and the wigs and heels weren't far behind. Becoming a "gender-dysphoric freak" struck me as a very natural progression.

Performing came naturally as well. As a little boy, I'd often tie a sheet between trees in our backyard and invite the neighbors over to watch my plays. I'm sure they were pitiful productions, but it's telling that, offering nothing, I was able to round up my sister and other kids in the neighborhood to perform. Since my dad taught at the University of Tennessee at Chattanooga, I was sometimes called upon to play the child part in college productions, too. Were these half-assed reviews the foreshadowing of Wigstock?

In *The Winter's Tale*, I played the prince. Wrong gender, but still royalty, honey! In grade school, I was cast in the school variety show as a snake charmer. If I could have looked into a crystal ball I would have seen that in the years to come I would "charm" many "snakes" indeed! I convinced my mom that slanted eyeliner, a la Barbara Eden on *I Dream of Jeannie*, would "exoticize" my look; together with a turban and harem pants, it might as well have been drag. I assumed that I'd continue act-ing, but when college hit and I was cast in the supremely dull *Our Town* as baseball player number two, I remember thinking, "I've been forced to act straight throughout high school. I'm ready for some more flamboyant parts—this isn't ME!" Plus, an actor is a mere pawn. A drag queen is able to be her own cos-tume designer, choreographer, makeup artist, hairstylist, script-writer, arranger, director, etc. So I have more input and control with what I do, not that I'm an impossible, controlling monster bitch or anything!

And why is Wigstock so important? Hmm. Well, the only thing worse than sounding pompous is an old battleaxe like me coyly batting her long, fake lashes in a failed attempt at false modesty, so let me brag a bit about starting Wigstock! In 1982, I moved to Atlanta to study at Georgia State, but who needs a degree to become the town drunk! Besides, I found the future superstar drag queen RuPaul and his cast of crazies far more interesting than the college curriculum of an undecided major. I tagged along on one of Ru's trips to perform at NYC's Pyra-mid Club and never left, rising from the ranks of go-go dancer to Wigstock organizer. I organized the very first one—an all-day drag festival of dancing and music and stage acts, including me as the emcee—in 1985. It was supposed to be a little trans-vestite festival and about a thousand people showed up! Every-one wanted to see or be seen or both. We had terrific acts every year, from recording artists like Deborah Harry, Deee-lite, and Vickie-Sue ("Turn the Beat Around") Robinson to big name queens like RuPaul, Lipsynka, and John Cameron Mitchell as Hedwig. Wigstock continued to grow and probably reached its zenith with the 1995 release of the thoughtfully named docu-mentary *Wigstock: The Movie.*

I am proud of several things. I was single-handedly responsible for the massive East Coast syphilis outbreak, for example—oh, just kidding—but organizing Wigstock is even more important than that. And it lasted twenty years, not a bad run for New York City. For a couple of years we had terrible weather—it's hard to clap and hold an umbrella at the same time—and we lost money hand over fist. At present we've stopped putting the festival on as an annual event, but who knows what'll happen in the future. Wigstock transformed people. It allowed me to bring a lot of zany, bewigged freaks together in the light of day for a very memorable annual blowout bash—even the somber *New York Times* wrote that "the karma was dynamite." And it allowed me to use my smart-ass humor—with the emphasis on ass, of course.

Illuminating the Truth

Sue Coe's work shocks and upsets people, in no small part because it encompasses such shied-away-from subject matter as the Ku Klux Klan, apartheid, Malcolm X, skinheads, AIDS, labor and sweatshop conditions, war, and animal rights. Her paintings are whole depictions, rather than glimpses, of what goes on in places most of us will never set foot in because we never, ever want to go there, physically or mentally. Once Sue Coe draws you inside them, through her work, any comfortable view of the world you might have had is whisked away. Somehow, too, her work is alive with sounds. Opening her book, Sheep of Fools, *I can hear the sheep boarding the multitiered, open-decked ships taking them to the markets of the Middle East; in* How to Commit Suicide in South Africa *I can even hear the escaping breath of the men who, because of the color of their skin, are sent plummeting into the abyss. The sounds aren't there on the page, but I hear them; that is how powerfully she paints.*

Sue believes her paintings are beautiful for reasons she explains in this verse:

Are these pictures all too dark for you?
Too much black? Too much blue?
Too much squalor?
Too much crime in this landscape of our time?
Then open your eyes,
X out their lies,
and work with your minds, your hearts, your sinews for a better world.

It would seem many people are keen to embrace Sue's "better world." Trained at the prestigious Royal College of Art in London, her work has appeared in numerous publications including the New York Times, *the* New Yorker, Art News, Time, Newsweek, *and* Mother Jones. *Her paintings have been included in the permanent collections of countless museums including the Metropolitan Museum of Art, the Museum of Modern Art, the Whitney, and the Arts Council of Great Britain. Yet in spite of all her acclaim, what Sue really cares about is telling the truth.*

Our house, when I was growing up, was in front of a hog factory farm, and one block away from a slaughterhouse. The pigs were kept in steel sheds. In front of the sheds was a chained German shepherd; he was chained for my entire childhood. The chain would rattle and get caught up in the dog's legs. Lights would go on in the sheds at night, illuminating our bedroom, and the pigs would start to scream. It was a very rundown place, and my sister and I were scared of the German shepherd. There were a lot of rats, and they would get the exterminator to come and put down poison. In the morning, we would find moles that had been killed, and would examine their soft fur and perfect paws.

One day, a small pig escaped the slaughterhouse, and she ran in and out of the traffic, desperate to get away. Men in white aprons, covered in blood, ran after her. Small groups of people congregated to watch, and they started to laugh and point. I asked my mother why this was so funny, and she said it was not funny, the pig was going to be caught and killed. My parents grew up in England during World War II and always told me that they didn't know about the death camps; what the Fascists had done came as a total shock. They survived the German bombs as teenagers, and because of this, everything in their lives was related to the war. Many buildings where we lived outside of London were still in ruins, entire rooms would be exposed, showing a fireplace, and photographs on the mantelpiece, staircases intact, but no walls. Our questions as children weren't really answered about how this could have happened, but even without their input I made the connection between the hell of the war and the hell of what was going on next door to us.

When it came time to slaughter the pigs, which would happen every six months or so, there would be a terrible noise at night. They'd whip the pigs to get them into the truck, and they would go down the road to the slaughterhouse. I wanted to know why this was happening, and my parents said this was "food" and to "grow up," and not worry about it. Yet here we were, living next door to a death camp, but for a different species. And then I started to understand why this could happen, how we humans can develop a mechanism to deny reality. Our behaviors are learned for the most part, and we learn early on as children that some lives are lesser than others. A spider web can be torn down, a mouse trapped, a frog dissected, a deer in the garden becomes a nuisance, a rat becomes "vermin," an undocumented worker becomes an "infestation." If we accept that some lives are more valuable and important than others, then we can be easily manipulated by corporations into killing total strangers in wars, and slaughtering billions of other animals for no logical reason other than profit and power for a tiny minority. Therefore, why not a pig?

When I was about ten years old, I went with my friend to the door of the slaughterhouse and demanded to be showed around, as I wanted to know what was happening. The workers in the slaughterhouse treated our request seriously, they were not patronizing, and they did show us around, they showed us everything that happens in the process of slaughter. The vision of the escaped pig couldn't be ignored; she became louder and louder in my mind, along with the sad chained dog, the mice that were kept in the school laboratory, the fishes in plastic bags, won as prizes at the fair, the old elephant at the traveling circus.

This experience as a child sent me on my lifetime's mission that was to be an artist, and to reveal what was being concealed. To get into places that have closed doors, and to give art the potential of changing the world, not just reflecting it. Truth is beauty, to me. If the art is honest, and shows the reality, then it is beautiful. As an artist, I have drawn in slaughterhouses, stockyards, prisons, AIDS hospices, night courts, and sweatshops. A pencil is not threatening to people, they can see what I am drawing, and can witness the process, and if they want the drawing, they can have it. I think that people don't want to go into slaughterhouses, because they say "there is nothing I can do about it," but what they really mean is they don't want to be a witness without power, because that would put them in the same position animals are in for their entire lives. To witness shocking events is to be traumatized on some level, and what artists do who depict these scenes is retraumatize the viewer. It's a way for the viewer who cannot gain access to a slaughterhouse, or prison, or miners' strike, or women's shelter, or canned hunt, or be in a war, all those sights we are denied by the mass media, to access that information at their own pace, without being told what to think. It's a way for the artist to share that vision and for the victims not to be alone; their voice is heard, even if it is by only one other. When I drew women in prison who had HIV/AIDS, I was frightened of the women, but then I realized that it was their lives that were frightening, not them. It only took a few moments to comprehend that I could be in their shoes, a few moments of reality to undo the propaganda we are fed. The seemingly conquered and oppressed are always kinder than the conquistadors.

Art does not happen until the viewer allows it to happen. If the viewer can observe in the work an investment of time and struggle for meaning, then there is a trust in the content. A simple pencil drawing can become the greatest tool for change in the world if it puts life before art. Art is a way of slowing time down, not speeding it up; it is the nature of art to be about progressive change, to grow alongside social justice struggles. There are very few great artists in history who we can say side with the ideology of fascism.

A Focused Lens on Life

When Susan Cohn was pregnant, she decided to make a film about the birth of her daughter, Annabel. The result, The Baby Shower, *became an award-winning documentary. Bitten by the filmmaking bug, Susan founded Jalapeño Productions, and went on to film* Green Fire: Lives of Commitment and Passion in a Fragile World, *which highlighted ten women who were granted environmental excellence awards by the United Nations Environment Programme. She has never stopped making films. She is also an author whose books include* Green at Work: Finding a Business Career That Works for the Environment *and* Finding Your Way with an MBA. *Her orientation is social justice and the creative arts, interests that have led her to be a board member of the Alaska Conservation Foundation, a foundation that works to conserve the ecosystems of Alaska and keep its communities sustainable and vital, and to serve as a policy advisor on Design Arts funding for the National Endowment for the Arts.*

What started out as a little diversion has blossomed into a most satisfying occupation. Susan Cohn's curiosity has not only taken her behind the camera but has opened countless other eyes and allowed filmgoers to accompany her on her exploration of unfamiliar worlds and other people's thoughts and cultures. Susan belongs in the book for proving that enthusiasm is sometimes all you need to develop a lifetime's journey.

Through documentaries, I believe that voices from underrepresented peoples or subcultures that have value but no feasible platform can come to life. And that all of society can benefit from such exposure. The more we can increase our knowledge and understanding of one another, the greater chance we have at being happy and productive. I tend to pick my subject matter based upon what I'm curious about, where my own questions are leading me. For instance, when I became pregnant with my first child I made a documentary about my baby shower. I came to realize that, yes, there are streamers, frilly dresses, and silly games involved, but beneath that there's a ritual of wisdom being passed down; that women steadfastly gather to help the mother (in this case, me) find grounding, peace, and strength in her new life. They do so by sharing their stories, stories of joy and stories of sorrow.

I'm also particularly drawn to individuals who are struggling to make a positive difference in this world. Early on, I made a documentary for Environmental Weekly (PBS affiliate distribution) about several women who'd been granted environmental excellence awards by the United Nations Environment Programme. More recently, I made a documentary about Richard Nelson, an activist anthropologist who's working to save the Tongass National Forest in Alaska. After college, I lived in Alaska teaching the Inuit people about organic gardening, so once more the draw to the subject matter was personal.

One of the most enjoyable and most bizarre documentaries I've made involved ultraruns. This is a modern marathon, where people run 100 miles in thirty-six hours or less. The elite runners do it in less than twenty-four. I found them fascinating: How did they train their bodies to endure such a grueling race, how did they train their minds, did they eat as they ran, were there bathrooms along the trails, did they run straight through day and night? Luckily, my former husband was one of them! So I brought along my camera and a crew to several key races and found a way to answer my questions.

I often have no idea what the ending of my films will be, but here, additionally, I wasn't even sure of what I was going to say. It was only through delving into the subject matter and trying to understand these people without judgment that the film came alive. I still receive e-mails about *Running Madness*. While sometimes thinking these runners are nuts, people are nevertheless inspired by the power of the human spirit.

I began making documentaries after writing my first book. Writing requires a lot of time spent alone, and although my book sold well, I felt that I wanted to stretch my artistic capacity into a visual medium. I had taken photography classes at the International Center for Photography in New York City and knew I had talent at framing and giving life to objects, plus after so many months shut away in my room, I thought a more collaborative environment would be fun. Friends in the business told me not to go to film school but rather to hire good people to work with me and, in a sense, apprentice to them. I took their advice, and for *The Baby Shower*, my first documentary, I hired filmmakers from NYU and a consultant who worked on feature films. All in all, I invested about $5,000, whereas film school costs about $40,000 and that's not including the money it takes to make a film! Together we created a documentary that went on to win at festivals and obtain distribution. This got me started. And with a bit of luck—and let me emphasize luck has a lot to do with everything in this business, along with connections—I was able to build my career from there.

Nowadays, documentaries can be made cheaply with the advanced technology available. And with highly watched Web streams such as YouTube, film-focused organizations like Witness (an international human rights organization that provides training and support to local groups to use video in their human rights advocacy campaigns), and the continually blossoming film festivals around the country, the odds of having your documentary seen have never been greater. These new communities create forums for better communication and a wider view of the world.

I believe in the old adage that if you change the mind of one person you can change the world. This isn't to say that documentaries should only be made about conventional social injustice. They can be about anything from some peoples' obsession with cats to mermaids to the use of scent in Proust's novels, whatever the filmmaker chooses. If it's done with intentionality, passion, and curiosity, it will impact the audience and encourage greater insight and empathy for one another. It's this increased kindness toward each other, based on increased knowledge of any aspect of human nature, that will bring about profound change.

HIS HOLINESS THE DALAI LAMA

Don't Worry, Be Happy

Tenzin Gyatso, His Holiness, the fourteenth Dalai Lama, is the spiritual and temporal leader of Tibet. He is believed by his followers to be the manifestation of Avalokiteshvara, the Bodhisattva of Compassion. He was born into a large farming family in the province of Amdo in 1935, and is said to have been watched over by a pair of wild crows, considered a potent omen. At the age of two, he was recognized as the reincarnation of the thirteenth Dalai Lama when regents from Lhasa organized a search party that led them to his village, based, as Tibetan tradition dictates, upon a series of visions and signs. The men tested him by placing some of the thirteenth Dalai Lama's relics on the ground in front of him. At the sight of the objects, the child cried, "They're mine!"

In 1950, at the ripe old age of sixteen, he was called upon to assume full power as Head of State, due to China's increasing military threat. Before he was out of his teens, he was entering into talks with Chairman Mao, and later, in hopes of finding support for his country, with Prime Minister Nehru. By 1959, he was forced into exile, having to cross the Everlasting Snows on foot and at risk of being shot, after the Chinese occupation of Tibet. I was living in New Delhi at the time and can remember that there were suddenly Tibetan refugees everywhere. Our dinner-table talk was of the revered man who considers himself "just a simple monk" (he went on to win the Nobel Peace Prize). Over the years, I grew to admire his advocacy of respect for all sentient life, his belief in altruism and unlimited compassion, his championship of harmony and understanding between different religions, and his view that all of us desire the same things: happiness and freedom from suffering. One reason, and there are many, that it is a delight to include his essay in this book is that he is a joyous person. And a very practical one. He points out that there will always be suffering and that if a situation is "fixable," there is no need to worry, and "if not, there is no benefit to worrying." He smiles and laughs because he knows he is doing all he can and that fretting serves no purpose! His contribution to this book is perhaps the most succinct and important message of all.

Compassion is one of the principal things that makes our lives meaningful. It is the source of all lasting happiness and joy. And it is the foundation of a good heart, the desire to help others. Through kindness, through affection, through honesty, through truth and justice toward everyone else, we also ensure our own benefit.

The necessity of love and compassion is the real basis of my religion, my simple faith. To put them into practice within a secular framework we don't need a temple, church, or other building, nor any complicated philosophy. Our own hearts and minds are where we work, while the only doctrine we need is compassion. So long as we put this into practice in our daily lives, so long as we have compassion for others and conduct ourselves with restraint out of a sense of responsibility, there is no doubt we will be happy.

Helping Children Find Their Feet

If you have seen the documentary film Mad Hot Ballroom, *or the feature film* Take the Lead, *starring Antonio Banderas as Pierre Dulaine, you have some idea of the impact this gifted dancer has had on children in the New York City Public Schools system. From shy bookworms to cocky delinquents, when children discover that they can move to music and start enjoying the experience, a transformation is often in the works despite their fierce initial resistance.*

Pierre, who until recently had been on the faculty of the Julliard School at Lincoln Center and the School of American Ballet, knows this because he experienced this same thrill himself, transforming from an awkward teen into a world champion ballroom dancer. Now he passes on this profound joy to children who might otherwise have only hung out in the streets or gone home to sit in front of the TV, who might never have discovered that their feet have wings, that they can win at something, or that winning isn't all that counts on the dance floor. His program reaches and teaches approximately 21,000 high school children every year. I love Pierre's story because his enthusiasm to teach is what makes the world go round, and not only under that magical ballroom dancing globe.

I was born in the Middle East, in Palestine. After that, I lived in Jordan, and then Lebanon, then off my family went to Birmingham, England. I was a very shy child, very timid, and to make matters worse, other children were quite mean to me.

They picked on me because I spoke with an accent, which they mimicked. But it was in England, when I was fourteen years old, that a school friend and I started taking lessons at the local dance studio. I was no good at dancing whatsoever, but something stirred inside of me and I loved it. So I persevered.

One day, I went to my very first professional dance competition, and I was awestruck by how wonderfully these professional couples danced. I clearly remember saying to myself that I would become a world champion dancer one day. And eventually, at the ballroom in Blackpool, England, I did. In fact, I won four times, starting in 1977 and including the "Duel of the Giants" at the Royal Albert Hall in London. My mother told me that I couldn't become what I wanted to be, a full-time dance teacher, because it would be too unreliable. She was nervous because we had been made refugees twice in the Middle East, so I can't blame her for worrying that this wasn't a "real" job. To please her, I tried working in an office, in accounting of all things, and I hated it. I became a hairdresser for a short time, but my sights were set on dancing. So, in London, at the ripe old age of twenty, I managed to get myself a full-time position as a dance instructor in a studio. It was difficult at times to make ends meet, very difficult, but I made it my profession, and I haven't looked back.

When something happens to you as a child, it becomes part of you. Dancing transformed me when I was young and timid. I knew it could do the same thing for other children who needed to shine in some way, to develop confidence in themselves. That was my raison d'etre for starting Dancing Classrooms in 1992. It's an ambitious program to teach dance to inner-city children, and I was met with blank looks and great skepticism when I first pitched the idea. It seemed bizarre and unworkable to many people in the school system back then, but they let me try it, and guess what? It worked.

And it doesn't just work in the classroom. Believe it or not, the children become better human beings because, through dance, they learn how to relate to each other politely. They learn manners and decorum.

I must say that these lessons, the whole experience of seeing children dance for the first time, of seeing them come alive, sometimes gradually, never ceases to amaze me! I see the looks on the children's faces. Their eyes almost pop out they are so wide when they realize they are having fun, that they enjoy dancing, that they are enjoying "shakin' what their momma gave them!" The way I work is to take them on a journey. They have no idea where they are going, but slowly they get drawn in and I see them loosening up and starting to enjoy themselves. And then it's too late for the ones who were acting up by saying they did not like it at the beginning. They are too caught up in it to go back! Their body language gives them away, and children really do tell it exactly the way it is. Each and every time I am in the presence of the children while they are dancing, I feel so blessed and so glad of having made my decision to volunteer to teach such classes in my first school fourteen years ago, before the school system truly welcomed me. The children themselves keep me motivated. That and my need to rediscover the passion that is inside of me, through them.

Banking for Babies

Can you imagine young children of four or five lying in the gutter, drinking from a trash-strewn puddle and sharing that drink with a family of crows? If not, you have never driven past the Dharavi slum in Mumbai, the biggest slum in Asia. As I did just that, on the way to Dr. Armida Fernandez's hospital office, I passed thousands of shacks made of cardboard and tin, all leaning against one another. Goats, birds, and children played and scrounged in the tiny filthy strip between these homes and the busy road to the Sion Hospital just beyond. They are banned now, but years ago, I saw a surreal sight above this sad and stinking place, a giant billboard advertising Nestlé's baby formula, something most of the over 1 million residents of the slum who live on a few cents a day could never afford. It wasn't until I met Dr. Fernandez, however, that I learned exactly how shocking the advertisement was.

Dr. Fernandez, a mother herself, has been so moved by the plight of the poorest children, especially newborns, whose mortality rate is unacceptably high, that she has dedicated her career to helping them in the most unique way, by starting the first human milk bank for babies in India. I included Dr. Fernandez in the book because I am particularly fond of India, a country I consider my second home, and because my own heart goes out to its poorest citizens, those she serves.

was born and brought up in India. My family wasn't keen on my becoming a doctor, but I was determined! After finishing my education at an excellent medical college here, I moved to a rural area where services were few and far between and joined a charity hospital run by nuns. One day, a child was brought in, and his stool had blood in it. I treated the child as best I could, but it was too late to help him at that stage, and he died. That was when I realized that the knowledge I had was not yet enough, and so I decided to specialize in pediatrics.

After that, I came to this crowded city of Mumbai and started working with a hospital in their pediatric department. Suddenly I was seeing so many newborn babies dying, many at less than a month of age. My colleagues and I discovered that most of them died due to infection that started as diarrhea. I presented a paper in which I analyzed the death rate of babies in Sion hospital. I'd found that out of 100 babies kept in the premature unit, 77 died. When I presented the paper, the delegates at the conference laughed at me when they heard these figures. On my return from the conference, I shared this experience with the Health Officer, who told me that this was a challenge and I needed to do something about the high death rate. This was the moment when I made the decision to devote my life to saving lives of newborn babies.

My colleagues and I started investigating the cause of all these deaths by conducting clinical studies. We learned that babies who were given prelacteal feed or animal milk formula by bottle had more chances of getting diarrhea than those who were fed their mother's milk. When I thought about that, it made sense. After all, human milk has everything a human baby needs for its physical, mental, and emotional growth. Besides, it has the right antibodies in it to protect against infection and diseases. If the mother is well, then she can feed the baby. But at Sion hospital, 40 percent of the mothers arrived with some complication or other; they weren't well at all. Many of the babies coming to us with these mothers were either sick or premature. So, although breast milk is best for the baby, when a mother is not in a position to feed the baby, how do we ensure that these children get the best milk that will help them grow and prevent them from getting infection?

We made a bold decision but a vital one. We decided to give all the babies in our care human milk exclusively and to stop the use of all other forms of milk. This was in the 1980s. At first, we used one mother to feed another mother's baby just like a wet nurse. If a mother had excess milk, we would extract the milk and keep it in the fridge and then feed premature babies with it, not very scientific. Nowadays, with the risk of HIV/AIDS, we cannot recommend wet nurses even in villages that still do not have milk banks. Back then, though, we had successes despite our primitive system. I remember one particular baby who came down with tetanus after being abandoned by his parents. He was very sick. One of our volunteers, a resident doctor herself, acted as a wet nurse and nurtured him back to good health. The orphan survived because of that volunteer.

Some years later, in 1987, I happened to go to the U.K., and I saw human milk banks where they extracted mothers' milk, pasteurized it, stored it, and fed it to needy babies. This method was extremely safe, and that was just what our babies needed. As soon as I got home to India, I started a milk bank at Sion Hospital. It was the first one of its kind in the country. Today, because of our milk bank, many more human milk banks have started. There are ones in Baroda, Goa, and two others in hospitals in Mumbai. That makes me quite pleased, as I know each one is helping children survive and grow strong, giving them an edge on life.

KATHY FRESTON

Becoming the Architect of Your Own Good Fortune

Kathy Freston is the sort of woman for whom it looks like life has just fallen perfectly into place. She is tall and good looking, beautifully dressed, highly personable, and a publishing success who is happily married to a man she calls "the one." What's more is that she radiates genuine happiness! On looking at her life now, it's hard to imagine that Kathy ever, in a million years, felt that she was a total failure. Yet, that is exactly how she viewed herself for many years.

What is remarkable about Kathy is that she didn't let experiences of rejection crush her; rather, she used them to deepen a growing compassion that she says connects her to anyone who is going through a hard time. She says that there is a certain intimacy people share upon experiencing a "dark night of the soul," and for this reason, her self-help books and CDs have struck a nerve and become bestsellers. Kathy is the author of Expect a Miracle: 7 Spiritual Steps to Finding the Right Relationship, The One: Discovering the Secrets of Soul Mate Love *and* Quantum Wellness. *I am so pleased that she is sharing her story and her "secrets" of transformation with you.*

I never had a strong sense of self; I didn't know if I was funny or smart or interesting or quirky. I felt rather like an empty shell always trying to fill in some ever elusive missing piece. I was always trying on different personalities to see what might

51

catch the interest of those I deemed superior. I tried being
cool, but just came off as being silly. I tried being super studi-
ous, but didn't have the attention span to keep up. And I tried
being athletic, but was sadly too uncomfortable in my body to
be coordinated in any sports. So you can imagine how I felt
when someone approached me to be a model when I was sixteen years old sitting with a boy at TGI Fridays in Dunwoody,
Georgia. I was stunned, and thinking the art director who gave
me his card must have left his glasses at home, I nevertheless
accepted an invitation to come in for "test" pictures.

At the studio a few days later, stylists poofed out my hair,
applied gobs of makeup, and pushed everything into the right
place. Then they blasted the lights so that you couldn't see my
pimples or freckles or chipmunk cheeks. Honestly, anyone could
look like a million bucks when put together like that. But the
pictures came out great, and off I went into a modeling career.
As lucky as I felt to be living in New York, Paris, and Milan,
I also woke up every day in fear that this would be the day they
would discover that they made a mistake and then boot me out
of the business. I simply couldn't see myself as one of those gals
who confidently strode the catwalk or pouted into a camera
lens with sultry knowingness. So when the agents began to
scold me for being too fat to fit the clothes and the photographers chided me to "loosen up" and move more deftly, I felt a
dark cloud of insecurity settle in around me.

The more I tried to fit in and be what the industry wanted
me to be, the more weight I put on and the stiffer I became in
front of the camera. One night I was just about to go to sleep
on the eve of a *Harper's Bazaar* shoot when my heart started
wildly palpitating and my skin began to crawl with intense fear.
I felt like I was tunneling out of my body and speeding toward
death. I could barely breathe as my mind raced with images
of myself in a world where I didn't belong. I ran down the

hallway of the hotel and pounded on the other model's door to tell her I was dying (I truly believed I was!) and needed to go to the hospital. Luckily, she was astute enough to realize I was having a panic attack and that it would pass. It did indeed pass, but for the next year or so I lingered in this dark place of feeling that I was on the verge of something terrible. It was during that time that I started reading.

I read everything I could get my hands on that would educate me on leading a deeper and more fulfilling life. I was swept up into the insights of Herman Hesse and Rainer Maria Rilke; I lost myself in wonder through all the diaries of Anaïs Nin; I found guidance in the Tao Te Ching and the writings of the current Dalai Lama; I discovered *A Course in Miracles*, Paramahansa Yogananda, and Joseph Campbell. Because I desperately wanted to know that there was more to life than being "pretty enough" or "hip enough," I turned myself over to these and many other tomes that became my teachers. I wish I could say that one religion or spiritual philosophy answered all my questions, but I never seemed to gravitate toward just one belief system. I was just grateful that as I learned about all these different aspects of life, the fear that had engulfed me seemed to lift.

Throughout the years that I continued to model, I went through a succession of relationships that seemed to fall short of my fantasies of what love could or should be. I dated alcoholics, control freaks, bar brawlers, and men who seemed to alternate between depression and volatility. One in particular was the guy who brought me to my knees. Although I was terribly attracted to him, this man was cold and abusive in every way—both emotionally and physically. I thought I loved him at the time, but now I look back and see that it was more of an addiction. Each time I broke up with him over some horrible transgression, I would slip into an obsession about how I should have handled things differently. So we went back and forth over several years, swearing off each other and then crawling back to each other when we needed a new "hit" of drama. We did this seven times. And with each return to the relationship, my self-esteem diminished more and more. By this time, I had nearly stopped eating, smoked over a pack of cigarettes a day, and had gone through my entire bank account since the modeling had dried up. I couldn't understand how this downward spiral happened until one day it dawned on me that my life was simply reflecting back to me my own self-loathing. I could read all I wanted, but unless I started embodying some of the wisdom I had gleaned from all those brilliant teachers, I would continue to feel ungrounded and "not enough."

So I turned my attention away from my failures (relationship, career, and health had all gone downhill) and started praying and meditating as per the methods I'd been reading about. I went to twelve-step meetings to address my addictive behavior. When I could afford it, I worked intensely with a therapist. I spent as much time outdoors enjoying nature as I could because everything seemed to become clear when I was away from city "noise." Then I started doing service: I volunteered at a place called Hollygrove, which is what used to be called an orphanage for kids who had been abused and neglected, and I took in a rescue dog named Beans. From that work, I learned to step outside of myself and see the bigger picture. I stopped wallowing in my self-centered fear and put my energy into helping to heal those who were suffering much worse than me. As I saw those kids begin to laugh again after the horror that they had been through, I realized that all of us have our crosses to bear and it's up to us to help each other out. Beans, the mutt who had been through God knows what before he got to me, taught me the greatest lesson of all: that happiness is attained by giving and receiving kindnesses.

It was all so simple really; I just had to learn to open my heart and extend my focus beyond myself. And wouldn't you know it, my confidence started building. I started feeling creative and inspired to try new and different kinds of jobs. My health started coming back, and friends told me I had a twinkle in my eye that had long since disappeared.

Practicing Harmony and Connectedness

Sharon Gannon founded Jivamukti Yoga School in partnership with David Life. It is one of the most well-regarded yoga schools and yoga methods in the United States. Jivamukti (which means living liberated) revolutionized yoga by reintegrating all of the aspects other modern forms had divided. She teaches all over the world (her students include Uma Thurman, Sting, and Trudie Styler) and has authored two books on yoga.

I always think you can judge a business by the mood of its staff, and there is such calm, kindness, and peace evident inside the Jivamukti studios that it is a reflection of Sharon's personality, which I have always found astonishingly, genuinely, and consistently loving and giving. Her path has inspired many people to seek their own.

When I was thirty and living in Seattle, I fell down some very steep and slippery stairs, fracturing my vertebrae, resulting in intense pain as well as intermittent paralysis of my right leg. I was a musician and performance artist at the time, without a lot of financial security, so seeing a doctor was out of the question. Plus, I'd recently suffered a personal trauma, which had led me to the brink of suicide. I'd come through it with an, at times, obsessive commitment to making something good out of my life. I'd also developed a high tolerance for pain and a no-tolerance approach to drugs, prescription or otherwise. Rather my approach was to continue with my daily activities regardless of whatever obstacles might appear. In fact, when there was difficulty I plunged into creative pursuits with a greater urgency, arising from a feeling that each day might be my last. It was with this surge of creativity that I moved to New York City to further explore my avant-garde artistic pursuits.

While I enjoyed my new home, the back pain wasn't diminishing; in fact it was increasing. I was waiting tables part-time, and a fellow waitress kept suggesting I take a yoga class. I found this advice to be silly and even annoying. I thought of yoga as just physical exercise and I was already getting plenty of that. In addition to waiting tables, I was also a bicycle messenger (I had to carry my bike up and down six flights of stairs every day), an aerobics teacher, a dancer, and a choreographer! Not to mention the strength it took to load and unload musical equipment for my gigs. So, I continued to do my best to ignore my body, but when the pain became so great that I could no longer concentrate, I went as a last resort.

During those first few yoga classes, I began to connect with myself in a radically new way. I had the rare opportunity of exploring the feelings in my body (I didn't even know my body could have feelings) and the judgments, assumptions, and opinions in my mind. Was it painful? Extremely so! But perhaps for the first time in my very physical life I was actually being physical. I wasn't trying to get out of my body, but I was going deeper into it with a sense of adventure. Previously, I'd objectified my body, viewing it only as a tool, because, after all, I was going to change the world and needed a body to accomplish this great work! Now I began to realize that ideas, even great ones, were not enough to change the world or to change my own life. Whatever I wanted to see in the world around me had to first become real in my own body right down to the molecular level.

To do this, I learned how to align with my breath. I discovered the only way that I was able to go deep into the pain in my back was by breathing. I couldn't think my way in, but only breathe. Breath is the life force; it is the Holy Spirit. It's what connects us all. Do you know that there are atoms of air in your lungs that were once in the lungs of everyone who has ever lived? We are breathing each other. There's a sense of deep relaxation and well-being when you actually feel that you aren't working against the world or the world isn't against you, when you feel that we are not only in this thing together but we *are* this thing together.

I began to practice regularly, and my back pain lessened. Initially, I had no intention of becoming a yoga teacher or of becoming the administrator of a large school with many other locations around the world. I still thought of myself as an artist. But when I got more deeply into the teachings of yoga, I realized that here was something that could help others understand how life works, how anything and everything works, how to be happy. The transition from East Village artist into yoga teacher wasn't a conscious one. It was an organic process. Many of the people who attended our performances (I was now involved with David Life and we were both performing art and practicing yoga together) knew we practiced yoga and would ask us about it. Eventually more and more people wanted to practice with us and not just sit in a seat while we did a performance. Of course, we continued to incorporate elements of our art into the classes, and we still do. Our trajectory is perhaps unusual in that we never went through a period of having to "recruit" students. We certainly didn't go about it all with a business plan. We knew nothing about business! We were poor artists, teaching in a basement on Avenue B, which we rented twice a week. Over the course of several years, I cocreated, along with David, the style of yoga called Jivamukti Yoga, which emphasizes the attaining of enlightenment through compassion for *all* beings; that if you want yoga, or enlightenment (the realization of the Oneness of being), then all of your relationships with others, which includes your relationship with the Earth, should be mutually beneficial, based in joy, and that this relationship should be consistent, not just when it is convenient for you. That is a powerful teaching! It could dismantle the foundation of our present culture, which is rooted in the notion that the Earth belongs to us. Unless you are able to live in a way that enhances the lives of others, you will not be happy; certainly you will not achieve enlightenment.

When I teach yoga, it's all of us involved in a communal effort to realign ourselves with the essence of who we all are ... the Divine Whole. In the Aramaic language there is a beautiful word for this: *Alaha*. It means all that is, referring to the individual, others, animals, plants, nature, and that which could be thought of as God. The practices of yoga refine your perception so that you see yourself as one with the whole. As a gentle, but potent, reminder to myself to keep Alaha in the forefront of my mind, everyday I wake up and say this Sanskrit mantra that David and I learned from Swami Nirmalananda during our first trip to India: *Lokaha Samasta Sukhino Bhavantu*. During the day, I remember it whenever I can. Swami Nirmalanada told us it means: May all be happy and free. Over the years of meditating on it, I have expanded on the translation, and so when I chant it I also add this in English: *May all beings everywhere be happy and free and may the thoughts, words, and actions of my own life contribute in some way to that happiness and to that freedom for all*. It's a powerful chant to teach because it reminds people of the power inherent in their own speech. If we say we want everyone to be happy, then we have to question everything that we do, how we live, how we eat, what we buy, how we speak. The best way to uplift our own lives is to do all we can to uplift the lives of others.

If you see something that's wrong and want to do something about it, first do your best to go to the cause of what you see, don't be content to deal with symptoms. This is a radical way to deal with things. The word *radical* comes from the same root word as *radish*, which means "root." Dig out the cause of the problem. Effective change can only occur if you change the course of action from the casual level. It's hard to face the fact that whatever problem we may see out there in the world is coming from inside of us. In fact, there is no "out there" out there, rather it's all coming from within us. Therefore, we become the change we wish to see in the world.

I have been practicing yoga and practicing being an open and mindful human being for many, many years now, and I've discovered that the true test of moral fiber is to stand for peace. To give up the love of power for the power of love. Peace will come when we have given up in our own daily lives hateful thoughts, cruel words, and violent actions. Cultivate hopeful thoughts, sweet speech, and kind actions. Let go of the need to exploit and hurt others to feel better about yourself. Whatever you want in this life you can have if you first provide it for someone else. Work for the freedom of others, and you yourself will become free. Don't wait for a better world. Start now to create a world of harmony and peace. It is up to you. It always has been!

JOHN GARDNER

A Vision of Physical Loveliness

John Gardner was in his late forties when he became blind. He wasn't prepared for it to happen. What he knew was that, somehow, he had to continue in his career as a physicist, although that wasn't going to be easy. In fact, if it hadn't been for his experience and effort, it might well have been impossible. John is an example of when "the blind leading the blind" can mean something extraordinarily positive. ViewPlus, the company he started, provides new tools for people with disabilities, including what some people are calling "the new Braille." This advanced system allows the blind to access data in many different forms and has revolutionized the field. When John lost his sight, he discovered what else was missing and set out to fill the gap. His determination to succeed is a terrific example of the power of one.

'd never had good vision. In fact, I was born with one functioning eye and I'd had glaucoma since childhood, but nevertheless I could see. I drove a car for thirty years! I like to joke that I didn't just get in and aim it, I drove it. I had absolutely no idea that I would go completely blind. Then, in my mid-forties, my functioning eye began giving me a lot of trouble. There was a problem with swelling, and fluid built up behind the eyelid. I had to put drops in it to keep the pressure down, but in the end that wasn't working. My doctor recommended a common operation to implant a pressure valve, and so I said, "Yes." The risk of something going wrong was tiny, so tiny I never even thought about it. You don't make decisions based on a one-in-a-million chance. After the surgery, the doctor made some calls, and most ophthalmologists he spoke to had never seen someone go in for such a minor operation and wake up blind before. But that's what happened to me.

I was already physically weak at the time, because pressure on your eye affects your whole body. I had lost twenty-five to thirty pounds and become as thin as a rail over the previous two to three months. It sounds odd to say, but I was so happy to be feeling better with the pressure gone that at first the fact that I was blind didn't register. I just wanted to rest and get well. It took several months from the time when I woke up in the hospital to the time that I knew that I would definitely never see again. No one wanted to tell me I was going to be blind forever. When that realization hit, I became very depressed, knowing I wouldn't see my future grandchildren's faces, or the sunrise, the sunset, the cities in Europe and Asia that I loved. Then, I thought of some people I knew who'd suddenly become disabled and how they were sour, bitter, and withdrawn. I felt sorry for them, but I didn't like them. I knew I didn't want to get like that. So I decided I wouldn't.

At the time I went blind I was a tenured physics professor at Oregon State University, running a physics research group of ten to twelve students and postgraduates and visiting faculty. All of a sudden, I wasn't there to provide guidance. It was September and our funding agency was threatening to cut off funds as they do at the same time every year, except this time I found myself fighting that recurring battle from my hospital bed. I remember thinking, "I could do without this!" Luckily, my colleagues stepped up to the plate and said, "We'll take your classes." They were great. No one but me questioned that I was going to keep on going.

I didn't know anything about being blind. I didn't know where to get the little white cane. One of the worst things was not being able to tell time. My father-in-law got me a talking clock, and later I found out about talking watches. But more than anything, I needed a way to communicate. My students were recording things on tape and a university reader would read me my mail and so on, which was helpful, but made me feel dependent. So I began studying Braille. I'd never used Braille before. All I knew about it was that it's made up of little dots. I learned it in a few weeks, which isn't hard to do. It's like learning basic piano. But it was slow, I had to keep stopping and thinking, and I wasn't exactly playing Rachmaninoff. The problem is that Braille is all about contractions, it's shorthand of a sort. The original Braille was punched out on a stylus. Then, when repetitive stress syndrome was identified (the realization that punching all those little dots is too much for a person), it became contracted, not everywhere—the Spanish and Italians and Swedes have a better system—but for English Braille you have to use contractions, which makes reading very arduous. When I discovered that blind people can use a computer it was a very happy day! It was only words, but it was something!

When it comes to math, there's a way with Braille to convert numbers into letters, but there are no symbols for such things as a plus, times, or equal. Letters are used instead, with "a" being "1," "b" representing "2," and so on. It's just impressions, and it's impossible to do serious math this way. I heard of a new computer that made heavy wax printings that you can feel, and I bought one, but the wax was sticky and came off on my fingers. Additionally, as a physicist, my real problem was graphs. Students have thousands of points plotted on a graph as a function of time, and all of a sudden I couldn't see the graphs, so I didn't know if they were good or bad. In the end, access to graphical information became the serious problem I couldn't overcome. I thought, "Why does this have to be so damned hard?" About a year after losing my sight, someone overheard me complaining during a visit to the National Science Foundation. He said, "If we give you $30,000, could you come up with a solution?" That began my new career.

Together with my graduate students, I developed a software and printer that was able to print Braille, mathematical symbols, and, most importantly, graphs. The letters and graphs are identical to what might appear in a book or magazine except they're larger and embossed so they can be understood by touch. Today you can read charts, graphs, and diagrams in Microsoft Word and Excel. You can even add a little bit to Math Editor, it's a five-minute job, and then you can print everything out on our machine. The first blind person I showed the system to was fascinated. She said, "Oh my, here is a fraction! And here's a numerator over the denominator. I've heard that, but I've never actually seen one! There's a radical sine. It's so easy to see what goes under the sine. It's wonderful!" Blind people of my own generation say, "Boy, if I'd had this when I was in college, I would have majored in science or in math." Now blind kids find that door is open to them, completely.

I knew this new technology could solve a host of problems not only for blind people, but for anyone. People with dyslexia are now using it, as are disabled folks who can see; it gives them alternative methods of access. I'd been quoting from a speech in which my friend, a teacher, had said that about 45 percent of all the information in any professional literature, in newspapers, even K–12 textbooks, was graphics. When I ran into her, I asked if I had that right. She said, "No more! Now it's about 75 percent. That's how kids get their information." So, the company I started, ViewPlus, makes this technology accessible. We're mainstreaming information, and pioneering ways to convert graphics information into a form that's the best one for everyone.

There is a motto I like very much. It's from the National Federation of the Blind, an organization that does a lot of good. It's, "Being blind is a nuisance." My aim is to make it a bit less of one.

Just Pick Yourself Up . . .
and Start All Over Again

Ah, the smell of motor oil in the morning! If you are a garage groupie and track hound like me, few things in life thrill you like those distinctive fumes or the sound of engines revving for a race. Andy Granatelli feels the same way, and he's been a hero of mine for decades. His nickname is "Mr. Indy 500," and if you don't know about the Indy, then that title and my car bumper sticker, "Free the Indy 500," won't mean a thing. But, if you know that Indianapolis is the most famous speedway in the world, you are also sure to know that Andy is a genius, one of the great legends of American motor racing, a man who not only designed some of the fastest engines ever to power race cars, but also set over 400 land-speed records. His name is also synonymous with STP, the motor oil additive company he bought quite cheaply in 1963 and made world-famous.

Andy Granatelli has done just about everything in racing, from taking apart the insides of the cars to designing and inventing parts of them, from being a driver to being a team owner. As fascinating as it is for me to hear him talk about racing and engines and about his drivers—among them the amazing Mario Andretti, Richard Petty (who won the Daytona 500 and the NASCAR championship seven times each), and British racing legends Graham Hill and Jim Clark—more important is Andy's rags-to-riches story that all came about because of his will to succeed. He embodies the "can do" attitude that makes America great. And not only can he do for himself, but he seems to have limitless ideas of what he "can do" for others. Andy has given, and continues to give, not only substantial amounts of money, but also time and boundless energy to nearly 100 philanthropic endeavors that encompass all aspects of society, including the arts, community health, local schools, medical and scientific research, alcohol and drug abuse, public safety, disaster relief, law enforcement, child welfare and development, and youth mentoring. When he sold Grancor (an automotive company he founded in 1945), he gave controlling interest of the company to his employees, free of charge. To use a racing metaphor, Andy's generosity extends from the starting lap to the checkered flag.

He is in his mid-eighties now, but his life's story is a timeless guidebook for living the American Dream.

My mother was killed when I was twelve. She worked hard, taking care of my brothers and my dad, who was sick a lot, and me. There were lots of problems. My father was an Italian immigrant who had to struggle to make ends meet. I knew what it was like to starve, to be hungry. Nothing in life came easily.

A lot of people think my dad got me into racing, but when they read something that they think is about my father, it's about me! We didn't have a car; my dad couldn't change a spark plug his whole life. That's not how I got started. What happened was that I was listening to the radio and the Indianapolis 500 race came on. It was 1935. When I heard those motors zooming around, I was hooked. That noise can do something to you. From that moment on, it was my goal to be around cars, to understand cars, to work on cars. I began tuning them for a dime just so I could learn. By 1945, my brothers, Joe and Vince, and I owned a gas station, Andy's Super Service, in Chicago. We worked very hard; we had drive in us. We built up a net worth of $30,000, which was a lot of money then. Then, one day, we went to work and there was nothing there. Nothing! Thieves had broken in during the night and hauled away all our equipment, all the tools, even our cars! All that was left were the four bare walls. We were cleaned out. That robbery left us dead broke.

I never give up. That's my motto. We started all over again right away, as if we'd never been there before. We started Granatelli Automotive Specialists. It was the first speed shop outside California, and within a year we had another $30,000 built up. Then there was a fire and the place burned to the ground. I started all over again. That's the story of my whole life. If you put in the effort, you can be what you want to be. Life is a big tug of war, but you must never let go of that rope, never stop pulling, and never stop. You have to have the right attitude, that's all. My brothers and I started taking engines apart and figuring things out from the moment we got started, and we never let anything hold us back.

My first car was a Model A Ford that I bought for $35. I loved it; it meant a lot to me. Since then, I've had hundreds of cars, and I always want to find out what makes them tick. Being an innovator, I've always tried different approaches. My cars always run something different than everyone else's, they're always special, with parts that no one had imagined before. I designed engines for Chrysler, Cadillac, and Studebaker. The Novi was the fastest car in its day, with a supercharged V-8 engine that you had to hear to believe. It ran at Indy from 1941 to 1966. I had a little money by then, so I stepped in and bought the rights, increased the horsepower, and put it back on the track in 1961, making it a four-wheel drive, and raced it for six years. Bobby Unser was one of my drivers. People will always talk about that car; it had such charisma.

In 1967, long after the auto shop days, my brothers and I had been working secretly on a revolutionary type of car, one with a quiet turbine engine. Nothing like it had ever been seen before, so we had to keep it under wraps until it was time to race. Then we wheeled it out, and the media went crazy over how radically different this STP-Paxton turbine car was. It looked good, it ran beautifully, and it was quiet as a mouse.

So, I've had a lot of success, don't get me wrong, but I think it's important for people to know who, at times, are struggling toward their own goals, that nothing ever came easy. There were always major obstacles and misfortunes, and it took work to turn them around. For instance, with the Novi, although it was the fastest car on the track, a car spun out in front of us and totaled the car. That was heartbreaking. We'd worked so hard; the car had even been in a garage fire and we'd got it built up again and put it back in the race. Another time, in 1969, my brothers and I built a very special four-wheel-drive Ford-powered Indy racecar. It took the fastest time on the track. It was going great when my other car hit it, demolishing both cars! I could have hung it up, given up, but that's not my nature. I try again. This time, we put the previous year's car back on the track and won the race by a full lap! There's no point in ever feeling sorry for yourself, you've got to fight to stay alive. If there's no effort, what's the point? If I give you a million dollars today, you'll be over the moon. But if I give you a million dollars every day, day in and day out, your whole desire will change; it won't mean as much, or much of anything, to you, will it?

Every year I take twenty-five to thirty people to Indy. I pay for a private jet, their hotels, the works; they give $50,000 each to charity, that's the deal. Often the wives don't want to come; they don't know what this Indy thing is, this obsession with cars going around a track. But, I tell you, when they hear, "Gentlemen, start your engines," and that roar begins, and then the biggest single crowd at any specialized sport in the whole world rises to its feet as one and roars back, they understand! And they want to come back.

Regrets? By the time my father died in 1977, I'd been in twenty-two Halls of Fame in twelve different categories, so he knew I was a success, but I still wish he had been around to see me being knighted by the president of Italy in 1994. That would have made his heart sing like one of my engines! More than anything, I wish my mother could have seen my achievements. It would have made her so proud. Throughout all the ups and downs, though, I never let depression enter my sights. I never look back in life, always forward. You could say I have no rearview mirror!

Thinking in Pictures

Dr. Temple Grandin has autism. She also designs slaughterhouse systems that reduce stress for animals killed for meat. Long ago, I went to Washington to present her with an award for leadership. Many people were puzzled how I could support Temple's work, given that PETA and I are anxious to stop people from eating animals. But I admire her. In a world where not everyone is ready to go vegetarian, she has relieved massive amounts of suffering through her innate ability to see, in her mind's eye, what "spooks" the cows and pigs who are herded into the chutes.

Temple is a scholar and a teacher (she studies and teaches at Colorado State University), as well as an author who describes herself as a "weird nerd." And it is what's inside her head that makes her stand out. By putting to use her "dis"ability to see in pictures, she has helped countless individuals, both human and non. She can teach us much because of that and because she has also single-handedly elevated the status and built the self-confidence of people with autism.

When I was in high school and college I assumed everybody thought in pictures the same way I did. I gradually learned that my thinking was different by interviewing other people about how their mind processed information. I asked them to think about a church steeple and discovered that some people only visualized a vague generalized steeple instead of the specific identifiable steeple pictures that I see. The ability to think in pictures is a real asset for a person who designs equipment. For instance, I can test run equipment in my imagination. I run a 3-D virtual-reality video in my head.

Visual thinking is probably more like how an animal thinks. There was no one single point where I discovered I could see and feel like cows, but some animals do not have verbal language so their thinking has to be based on associations between visual images, sounds, and other sensory-based memories. Having thought patterns that are more like that myself makes it easier for me to understand them. Likewise, my achievements in the livestock industry are not the result of a single event but a long, steady progression of work over thirty years.

When I first started talking about thinking in pictures, some twenty years ago, many autism professionals thought it sounded crazy. Recently, I had my brain scanned with the latest scanner that can map larger brain circuits. I found that I have a huge cable in my right hemisphere that goes from my primary visual cortex up to my frontal cortex. It's almost twice as thick as the one in my sex-age-matched control scan, which supports the notion that people on the autism spectrum really do think in pictures. What interests me most in this type of research is consciousness, both in my autism and my animal work. To me it was always clear that animals are conscious; therefore, when I started my work, it seemed obvious to me to get down into the chute and see what the cattle were seeing. Not only seeing, but feeling as well. People with autism often have body boundary problems. We don't know where we end and, say, the chair we're sitting in begins. This served me well in the chute, because I was able to experience the machine as an extension of my limbs. Because of this, I could "feel" the cattle and know how much pressure was the right pressure, a comforting pressure, one that wouldn't panic or hurt them during their last moments of life. I believe in a hereafter, and I believe animals have souls, so this time with them was extremely precious, and being able to make this work properly was like a religious experience. Naturally, being involved with watching the animals die made me look at my own mortality. When you look at your own mortality, you wonder about the meaning of life. When it becomes my time to die I will ask myself "Did I do something to make the world a better place?" Looking at your own mortality is a great motivator to do something of value.

But doing something of value isn't always easy. Early in my career, I was a very nervous speaker. In fact, in 1970 I was supposed to teach psychology class during my first year of graduate school, but I became so nervous that I walked out. I realize now, one of the reasons I panicked was I had no slides. And I needed them to help make the pictures that were so clear in my head a reality for others. This was an important realization for me because I knew I wanted to actively bring about change rather than simply heighten awareness of it. For instance, Zen meditators are able to achieve a state of oneness with the universe, an acceptance of reality as it is, but I wanted to reform aspects of reality. The dreadful shackle hoist system would still exist if I'd not been involved in convincing the plant to remodel. Therefore, identifying what was tripping me up and figuring out a way to work with it was vital to achieving my vision.

In 1974, I started doing cattle-handling talks. Since I was a weird nerd, I had to show a portfolio of my work to convince people that I was skilled. I learned about the power of showing a portfolio when I was at a meeting of the American Society of Agriculture Engineers. Since they thought I was weird, few people wanted to talk to me. The attitude of many of the engineers toward me really changed after I showed them one of my drawings. They said, "You drew that?" People respect ability, and there are other people on the autism spectrum who've had successful careers by selling their work instead of themselves. I encourage other autistic people to show what they can do, rather than wait for people to come to them. Autism is who I am, and by talking and writing about how autism has helped me with my life's work, I strive to give others with autism courage and confidence. Ideas are passed on like genes, and over the years I've discovered I have a great desire to pass on my ideas. I would like for everyone, autistic or otherwise, to experience this same pride of helping other beings, to feel the same satisfaction I get when I see that I've changed something that was once awful into something that is now good.

Defending Whales and Seals

While Peter Hammarstedt is only in his early twenties, he is already a driven man, a sea warrior who works aboard the mightiest antiwhaling, antisealing vessel in the oceans, the Sea Shepherd. *He is also the first mate aboard the* M/Y Robert Hunter, *what he describes as, "the newest addition to the Whales' Navy." I wanted Peter in this book because he illustrates very well how rewarding it is to follow your heart and have a huge impact on those with no voice. I spoke to him at his home in Sweden, where he was born, but Peter and the* Sea Shepherd *are seldom there. Their work is off the bloody ice floes of Newfoundland, in the waters off the coast of Japan's dolphin killing fields, and guarding Mexico's turtles from human predators.*

Growing up I was a bit of a loner, although I have a younger sister. We moved constantly, so I didn't have steady friends. I lived eight months in Kuwait, going from snow to sand, then two years in Saudi Arabia. At the age of five we moved to China; at six I was living in England; at seven we moved to the United States.

Because of this, I was always sensitive to what was going on in the world. One of my very earliest memories is of my mother yelling frantically for me to get away from the windows. It was the Tiananmen Square massacre. The troops were shooting at the windows, knowing we were foreigners, trying to make sure, I suppose, that we didn't look out and see what they were doing to the students and other people on the streets. In thinking back, I believe that more than anything, this is when I learned that we live in a world where humans believe that "might makes right." We had to pack up as quickly as possible and get out. As we were leaving, I saw tanks everywhere. I was allowed to take only one thing. I chose my toy dog, Dizzy, and I still have him.

Back then, I wanted to be all traditional things, like a doctor, a priest. When I was about twelve, I started giving 50 percent of my allowance away to charities. Once, I saved about $100 and I had to figure out what to do with it. I started looking up different animal protection groups on the Internet. That's when I came across a picture of Antarctica, and it was a life-changing experience. After that, there was nowhere else I wanted to be but in a Zodiac (an inflatable boat) protecting whales.

The first vegetarian I met was a girl in my class in Pennsylvania. A group of kids surrounded her desk and were giving her a very hard time, asking her would she eat this or eat that, lots of silly hypotheticals. She was calm. I accused her of trying to take away my "right" to eat meat. The girl said no, she was just trying to enlighten me. She explained that on a factory farm, a hen lives her whole life in a cage just eight and a half by eleven. My jaw dropped. I didn't eat lunch that day, thinking about what that must be like. I knew that if what she said was true, I couldn't say I cared about animals but still eat them. I felt betrayed that no one had told me this before.

There is a painting on my wall that my mother took out of China when we evacuated. At that time, any art was illegal in China if it was not Communist art, and there used to be illegal art shows in homes in the countryside. That's where she bought this one. It shows thirty hens pecking at grain, and it means a lot to me now. It hangs right beside my "I am not a nugget" poster showing a little chick who doesn't want to grow up to be inside a KFC box! I think my mom recognized my track in life before I did.

I found I could never shake those original images of Antarctica and the whales, so, as I grew into my teens, I began doing some research. I came across the *Sea Shepherd* site and read that the ship was looking for crew. By that time, I was old enough to leave home so I signed on right away.

The Canadian seal slaughter that I witnessed still gives me nightmares. People call it a "hunt" but I have yet to meet a single hunter who would call bashing baby seals over the head with clubs, "hunting." I was there in 2005. The ice is absolutely surreal, heavenly, like a world made of broken fragments of mirrors that sparkle in the light, that reflect the colors of the rising and setting sun. It is a wonderland where mother seals come to have their babies, to leave them to bask in the sun, feeling that they are totally safe, being miles and miles away from man. Not realizing that the boats will come, that human greed will catch up with them and reduce them to a bloody pulp.

Humans don't belong there at all. We must go there to confront the seal killers, to film what they do, to report their indefensible acts of unspeakable cruelty to the world, to witness their despicable acts that violate the International Seal Protection Act. We see an entire world of white turn to red as the seals' blood runs across the ice. There are suddenly carcasses everywhere as the babies are killed with the blunt or sharp ends of the Hak-a-piks, and stomped, kicked more than once, sometimes six times or so with the sealers' cleated boots.

During the hunt, I found myself running from the Royal Canadian Mounted Police. They're there on the ice to protect seal killers, not seals. I had video evidence, and I didn't want them to seize it. But they tackled me and knocked me to my stomach. I lay there, practicing passive resistance, my arms held behind my back. And as I turned my head, there, just two or three meters away, was a pup. I was so close to her, and her eyes and my eyes were linked together. I do believe she knew the difference, she knew I was not a sealer. As long as I lay there, she was safe.

On a good day, we can stop sealing, but the hunt is massive, and they keep coming back. When I know I have saved a seal, it is an extremely personal experience. I don't care then if I am locked up for years! We're often assaulted, but we have to stand our ground. Our clients are the marine animals who have no way to fight for their lives; no power. I think Captain Watson (founder of the Sea Shepherd Conservation Society and founding director of Greenpeace Foundation) speaks for all of us, whether we are on the ice floes or the high seas. When he was challenged about sinking an empty whaling vessel in Iceland, he said, "The hell with you. I didn't do it for you. I did it for the whales. Find me a whale who would disagree and I'll stop." These sea animals have real intelligence, which means they absolutely want to live in harmony with the world. Even the "stupidest" of animals wants that. Captain Watson was once confronted by a whaling boat captain who told him that the reason it is acceptable for human beings to slaughter these magnificent mammals is because "we" have moral reason and intelligence. Captain Watson just stared at him. What is the good of reason and intelligence if all you do is use it to harm others?

RU HARTWELL

Global Flight Control

One look at the long lines at any airport, or at the newspaper ads for low-cost exotic vacations, shows that the skies are full of fuel-guzzling aircraft. And for every 750 gallons of fuel used on one of these flights (about the amount of fuel it takes to get one from Denver to Tucson), nearly 5,000 pounds of exhaust per hour is pumped into the upper atmosphere. Pretty frightening. Flying as much as I do, I find myself constantly looking down to see more and more acres of woodland disappearing, something that fills me with horror. Every tree is home to countless forms of life, and every tree felled means dirtier air for all the Earth's inhabitants—not a great prospect.

Ru Hartwell is a gentle and kind man who lives in the woods in the Cambrian mountains of mid-Wales. He loves trees and always has. Now, he has found a way to put his life's interest to work to help the environment and make people feel a little better about their trips. Through his firm, Treeflights, anyone boarding an airplane can partially mitigate their carbon footprint by sponsoring the planting of a tree, or several. It's an idea that's really "taking off" and a grand example of how doing what you love can make the world a better place, which fits the theme of this book to a T.

I've been a tree planter for a very long time as well as a frequent passenger on planes. In my youth, I traveled to forty-two countries. Back then, there was nothing I loved more than getting on an airplane in one location, soaring through the skies, and landing somewhere new. It's funny, although I loved trees then as much as I love them now, I wasn't connecting how my pleasurable flight here or there was damaging, often destroying, the very thing I loved most. When we fly, we create all this CO_2, the very antithesis of what a tree does. A tree absorbs CO_2, holds on to it and keeps it safely out of the atmosphere, to put it simply. It was just ten years ago that I heard the phrase "carbon neutrality," which means neutralizing the effect of the greenhouse gas emissions you are personally responsible for. I was very struck by this concept. Parent forest trees (not the constantly "harvested" forests that get replanted by, say, lumber companies) absorb very large amounts of CO_2, and the whole world's forests absorb 20 to 25 percent of all carbon emissions the world's industry spews into the atmosphere. We humans forget how amazing trees are. We take them for granted, perhaps because they are quiet, they don't make any noise. They are just there, doing an incredible job.

This conundrum began to bother me, and I spent a long time thinking about how to fix it but not getting anywhere. People, while perhaps cutting back on flights, aren't going to give them up altogether quite yet. Then, one morning, I woke up with this word having popped up in my head. Not just the name, Treeflights, but the phrase, "Click here to make it a Treeflight." I kept saying it, and I liked the sound of it. It signified so many different things. I told my sons about this idea when we were eating breakfast. My boys have every reason to discount my sometimes daft ideas. One earlier business idea was Christmas tree rental. I would dig up the tree, deliver it to someone's house for the holidays, and then return it to its patch afterward. The problem is that the trees didn't like coming from the Welsh mountains to sit indoors by a radiator. They coped, but they didn't like it, and it sometimes took them four to five years to recover from the experience, so I stopped that.

I believe that you can't have success and good feelings without failures and bad feelings. Losses bring you strength, and I've had plenty of failures and mistakes! But, when I told the boys about Treeflights, instead of ribbing me, they liked it. In fact, everyone I mentioned it to said, "fantastic!" I'd found something I not only deeply believed in, but a good thing everyone could really appreciate. The idea is that if people are booking a flight online through an airline Web site, they should be able to "click here" to make partial amends by sponsoring the planting of a tree, maybe two trees or more, depending on how much they wish to pay. I know it's hard for some people to stop flying, so planting a forest will definitely help mitigate the damage.

Sixteen years ago, when I first moved to where we live now, there were only four or five patches of woodland. The rest was windswept bleak pasture. Now our cottage is completely hidden in the woods. The area has changed for the better; there is wildlife and a real ecosystem, all thanks to the trees. To me, it has been a privilege to transform it all by planting them. The kids can enjoy playing outside. And the trees provide homes for the birds and insects and make an amazing wind break, without which anyone out here would be swept off their feet. I've always tried to live a green life, which is what trees are all about. We generate our own power in our small mountain retreat. We make electricity from the little stream, we have solar panels. So now that we've done that, I can dedicate myself to helping others reduce their carbon output, too.

For years now planting trees has been the main thing I do. In the last twenty-five to thirty years, I must have planted over 17,000 of them. I see trees I planted long ago that are so big now that I can only just get my hands around them, trees that are twenty-five to thirty feet tall. Of all those I've planted, fewer than twenty haven't survived.

It feels wonderful to know that they will outlive me. I feel better when I'm around trees. Growing up, I lived in London. My parents quarreled a lot and were sometimes absent, so I ran around by myself in some really rough parts of the city. When I was about eleven or twelve years old, I went camping in the Welsh countryside, miles from anywhere. I was in awe. The mountains and fresh air were such a contrast to the grimy parts of London. At some point, my parents moved into a ramshackle farm, determined to be self-sufficient. That's when I started planting trees, to help them out. I instantly knew that planting trees fit me.

My favorite tree is probably the humble little birch. People tend to ignore it, but I've planted a lot of them. They are robust, vigorous, quick growers, they can cope with almost anything, and their foliage is fantastic. They show an iridescent green leaf in spring, and in autumn they give off golden hues. They are truly beautiful. I plant them and the other trees with my hands, down on my knees with my hands around roots. I use a shovel or spade, dig a hole, spread the roots to make sure it's comfortable in there, and put dirt around the tree to give it food early on.

In the years ahead, I believe there will be an increasing understanding of the need to offset auto and flight emissions by planting trees. In the future I think flying will be seen the way smoking is seen today; or at least flying without arranging for some offset will be looked upon as wrong. As kids, we never thought about some things we know are problems today. Human behavior can be so selfish and destructive; we can't keep putting our hands in the cookie jar. Everyone must get on the path to doing less and less damage. The way things are going, we must all start to offset, and it will become de rigueur.

The program is expanding and I feel immensely privileged and lucky every day to be able to advocate for the trees. If people want to do Treeflights in countries outside Wales, I'm all in favor, but it won't be me setting it up because I'd have to fly there, and that would be counterproductive, wouldn't it! Now I'm in my late forties and seeing my children gives me all the pleasure in the world. I'm a bit like a tree, I suppose, quite content to stay at home, be still, be quiet, and be immobile.

A Burning Desire to Connect

It may take a village, but these days there is no village, at least not in America. That sense of a closely bound community has been lost as we drive about sealed in our cars, "talk" to each other over the Internet, work in our cubicles, and often do not know the names of our neighbors in an apartment block of hundreds of other souls. Larry Harvey is the founder of Burning Man, an annual event in the desert of Nevada, 100 or so miles north of Reno. Here, tens of thousands of people from every conceivable walk of life congregate every summer to become residents of Black Rock City, a temporary community where one of the rules is that no one may buy or sell anything. It is not a statement against commerce but against the "commodification" of imagination. Burning Man is often a life-changing lesson in getting along, in interconnectedness and the liberation of your soul. Larry Harvey's vision now extends to China, South Africa, and all over the world as the ridiculously simple yet phenomenally liberating idea of burning a large stick-figure man in a wide-open space catches fire in people's imaginations. He belongs in this book because he has used the idea of "one can make a difference" to empower thousands.

I can't think of anything more immediate, more accessible than burning a human figure. I mean, you could burn the figure of a tortoise, but you can't get in touch with your tortoise-self very easily, can you? But watch a man go up in flames, and something happens inside you. I discovered this about twenty years ago on a beach in San Francisco. I wanted to do something cathartic over a relationship, to heal my broken heart, so my friend Jerry and I built a human figure out of scrap lumber and hauled it down to the beach, poured gasoline all over it, and set it on fire. We didn't have a permit. It was impromptu and spontaneous and, as far as we conceived of it, a one-off gesture. Then people came running.

The flames rose like a second sun brought down to this earth. They transfixed us. Someone started singing a song about the fire, a hippie with a guitar, then a woman ran toward the figure. The wind had suddenly shunted the flames to one side. She took its hand on the other side and held it. We felt an immediate bond with these strangers. A day or two later when Jerry and I discussed this, I sensed that if we'd gone to a friend's backyard or to a formal exhibition space, it wouldn't have affected us so deeply. We'd made this happen in the company of people whom we'd never met, and their response seemed so authentic—immediate and unconditional. Subconsciously, I think this made us feel that we'd encountered something larger than ourselves. The Man grew out of that.

When people ask what Burning Man means I tell them you need to discover that for yourself. That's your task; you have to find the meaning it has for you. If you haven't been to Burning Man, it's difficult to explain the transformational aspect. Many people discover themselves there, discover what's inside them that needs to come out. You take it on faith that it'll happen if you heed the call. Nine times out of ten, people will say, "It changed my life." I hear this constantly. People also say, "I loved the art," or "I met some wonderful people." Another thing I hear a lot is "I went home and quit my job." This is a good thing. People find out that their job didn't fit them, that they were contorted by that job, that it crippled their vitality. They say, "I found something that suits me better."

America was founded on independence, on liberty, but today the experience of community is disappearing from our society. Kids often have no idea what civics is. They've grown up in a landscape that is littered with big-box stores, commercial strips, and shopping malls, so they view society as one big vending machine. That kind of lifestyle has isolated us from life itself. You can conduct all of your affairs via a credit card, but that isn't a connective experience: it's an abuse of the principle of freedom. It comes with lots of liberty, but it reduces social capital. If you extract people from this environment and drop them into a city—Black Rock City—that generates millions of creative social interactions, it's like heaven on earth to them. At first, of course, it can be frightening to people: arriving in a wide-open desert, surrendering their ego to a void. But, if you can do that, you can open your heart. Many people are afraid they'll hemorrhage if they open up their hearts; it's a threat to their survival. Very often, we refuse to open our hearts until our pain is so great that it's the last choice we have. At Burning Man, we create an environment where you can open your heart easily and it needn't involve pain, unless you count the rigors of wilderness camping. It produces personal expression, communal involvement, and civic enthusiasm, not pain!

All that I do now comes from my childhood, from my earliest experiences, moments that are charged in my imagination with a numinous power. When I cast my mind back, all the things that engaged my imagination then inform what I do now. As a child, I didn't just play with toy dinosaurs, but built interactive theme parks around them. I planned these out in very practical detail. In school, I was a pint-sized impresario. I rounded up my classmates, identified their talents, and directed them in performances that eventually appeared before the whole school. One of my earliest memories is of sitting in a large open trailer. My older brother had assembled walls within it out of orange crates. They were stacked three, maybe four, courses high, yet to my eyes it might as well have been the Halls of Montezuma. Then rain came bucketing down and everyone fled. I lay there on the floor of the trailer, looking up, thrilled by the oncoming storm and the sheer monumentality of it all. Now I've helped create a city that is full of things that are not only monumental—in the emptiness of that flat land-scape, they appear three times as tall as they really are!

Kids today should be taught that there's a greater world of possibility and that the opinions of those around them don't necessarily matter; they should be encouraged to ignore the pressure put on them to fit into the slot society affords them. We are beings, created things, each of us ineffably unique. How could conventional society possibly offer us enough choices? What did Freud say about Heinrich Schliemann discovering the site of Troy? Children of that era played with little metal soldiers, imagining themselves as ancient Greeks upon the field of battle. He said that Schliemann must be among the happiest of men on Earth. Freud thought that there is no true happi-ness in life except for the realization of a childhood wish, and I believe he was right.

I was always a lover of art and a voracious reader, but not being trained as an artist, not thinking I had "permission" to create art, I didn't. My standards were so high that I didn't want to do something that might fail. Then, living in San Francisco, I fell in with a Bohemian group of carpenters. One played Fla-menco guitar and painted pictures, another was working on a novel. We drank wine together, had fun together, and they taught me what San Francisco teaches a lot of people: self-expression is good for your soul. They helped me to relearn what I'd known as a child: it's possible to do things passion-ately, simply for the sake of doing them. You can let your spirit ventilate and move out into the world and see what happens.

Suddenly, I had permission to create, and I stopped worrying about what others might say. Since then, I've made it a practice to relentlessly bring things out of myself and toss them into the world. I'm a fantasist, but anyone can creatively express himself. Anyone!

You must have faith that there's a world out there that fits your innate gifts. It's all a matter of persistence. Your ideas may be wrong: you must be ready to accept that fact and try again. But don't avoid pursuing your visions because someone says "that's silly," or "that makes no sense." Often, it's these very people who are most disappointed with their own lives. One day, perhaps by happenstance, you'll arrive at a place where all that is within you matches all that is without. Whenever that happens, the vision that's hovered before you, so often indistinct, will vividly snap into focus: everything will be animate, everything will feel real. You will be living the authentic life that you were meant to live. Burning Man is simply a context, a framework that allows this to happen. The rest is up to you. It always is.

Sitting, Thinking, Creating, Saving

I am including Dr. Heimlich as an essayist because I not only admire him and have enjoyed knowing him personally—he is full of good jokes and clever thoughts and is staunchly opposed to animal experiments—but because he has saved countless people's lives. In fact, while the Heimlich maneuver has saved the lives of celebrities such as Cher, Goldie Hawn, and even former president Ronald Reagan, it also probably saved mine.

One morning I was, as usual, doing too many things at once, dashing about in the office, eating a breakfast sandwich, and putting paper in the copier, when I choked. It was early and only the man who vacuums our carpets was in the building, somewhere downstairs. I suddenly realized how difficult it would be, even if I could find him quickly, to get him to understand that my airway was blocked, that I couldn't breathe. Drawing on what I remembered of Dr. Heimlich's advice, I thrust myself forward, with force, over a chair. That action dislodged the bit of sandwich and I could breathe again.

Of course, everyone knows Dr. Heimlich for the Heimlich maneuver (and if you don't have a "How to Do the Heimlich Maneuver" poster in your office, please see the Resources section in the back of the book and get one from the Heimlich Institute right away), but there is yet another way in which he has changed the world for the better, and it began by his method of simply sitting and thinking about a possible solution to a problem that came to his mind.

Looking back, I suppose there were always indications that I liked to think about things and that I liked to create. As a child, I would dismantle an old umbrella and make a sword out of the wire bits, that sort of thing. My mother laughed about how I would sit very quietly for hours alongside the little brook that ran in front of our house. My mother would give me a rod fashioned of something or the other with a bit of string dangling from it, but my sister told her I wasn't fishing, I was thinking. In fact, everything interested me, and every place; I found meaning in most things.

In my teens, I was admitted to Cornell Medical College a year early, which didn't often happen. And, back then, only about four Jews were allowed in out of about eighty to 100 students admitted each year, so I was surprised. In World War II, I became a Navy doctor. Although I had joined the Navy because I liked sailing, I ended up in one of the driest places on earth: the Gobi desert of Inner Mongolia! That is what I jokingly call a "typical Heimlich maneuver." We had an old Dodge truck that carried a layer of 100 gallon gas tanks, then a layer of goods the driver was selling, then a layer of sleeping bags, and we traveled sitting on top of the bags. In the weeks it took to reach our headquarters in the desert, we visited ancient cities and met the last of the warlords. Our purpose: The weather in our location took three days to reach the Pacific; therefore our weathermen radioed a report daily to the Pacific fleet command enabling them to plan air and sea actions. My orders were to keep the Chinese on our side, since they had been occupied by the Japanese for nine years. I did that medically by treating hundreds of the local population. We were behind enemy lines, therefore we were protected by 250 Chinese soldiers. One day, I was presented with a young Chinese soldier who had been shot in the chest. Then, and for years after, a chest wound on the battlefield was a death sentence; there was nothing anyone could do. The lungs collapse and that's it. (In a hospital, a tube is inserted into the chest and it is attached to a regulated suction apparatus.) He died in my arms. Feeling terribly depressed, three of us rode out to the nearby village on our little Mongolian ponies to get something to eat and because I wanted a drink—they served Bi Jo, white wine—to take my mind off the situation. As we sat there, I spotted a pony trap (an open transport cart pulled by horses) in the distance. It had a wooden coffin on the back of it and I realized it had to be "my" soldier.

I didn't know I would become a thoracic surgeon then, but I returned home and took a residency and, in 1950, became one. It was so early in the game, in fact, that I was only the 139th surgeon to be so certified. I kept thinking what to do about chest wounds. I started to research different valves, because it occurred to me that it was really a valve that was needed to let the blood and air out, get the lung up and inflated, and keep it that way. I could see that the ball valve wouldn't work because if it was turned sideways it would fall open; that the spring on a flap valve closed it, but a clot of blood could hold it open. In either case, air would fill the chest and collapse the lung. Then I hit on the flutter valve; it is always closed, even when air or a clot are passing through it. Back then we had a thing kids played with called a "Bronx Cheer," it made a raspberry sound if you blew into it. That was a flutter valve. So I bought one at the five-and-dime store, sterilized it carefully, and attached it to a chest drain tube. When a patient was admitted with a collapsed lung due to pneumothorax (air in the chest due to a burst air bubble on the lung), I put the sterile tube into his chest. I stayed with him all day, taking occasional x-ray pictures, and the lung came up and stayed up. It was a success!

I took the idea to a medical instrument company I knew, and they immediately started manufacturing the Heimlich chest drain valve. In 1964, I presented the chest drain valve at an American Medical Association Convention, and a U.S. Navy commander, from the Navy Medical Research Institute came up to me, took six of the valves and flew to Vietnam the next morning. A week later I got a telegram saying, "The Heimlich chest drain valve is a life saving device. Must have 100 immediately." The demand increased terrifically, but the valve was being made by hand and there were complaints that they were not being made fast enough. Eventually, that valve saved hundreds of our soldiers in Vietnam. The beauty of it is that this valve is easy to understand and simple to use. You don't need a doctor; you don't need a nurse. In the end, every soldier ended up carrying the valve attached to a chest tube in a sterile envelope. If they got shot in the chest, they didn't need to see a doctor or corpsman. Their buddy inserted the tube into the chest through the bullet hole and it would do its job, getting the air and blood out and inflating the lung.

In 1993, years after the war, I was invited to Vietnam. When I got off the plane in Hanoi, Vietnam's head surgeon was introduced to me. He said, "Dr. Heimlich needs no introduction. Everyone in Vietnam knows his name." I thought he was referring to the Heimlich maneuver. Then he said, "The Heimlich chest drain valve saved tens of thousands of our people. Dr. Heimlich will live in the hearts of the Vietnamese people forever." I broke down and cried outright. Every year, over 100,000 Heimlich Valves are now used throughout the world, mostly for civilians. It is most gratifying to have thought about this problem and created a solution.

Change Is Healthy,
Change Is Good!

Dana Hork is a modest and understated young woman. When she was nine-teen and a student at the University of Pennsylvania, a thought came to her out of the blue. I find the compellingly simple story of how she developed her little gem of an idea—a sort of "add inspiration and it will grow" success story—per-fect for this book. The brilliance of it is that the fundamental thought of how to make something so good out of so little can easily be repeated in innumerable other scenarios. Dana shows us that all we need to do is cast about our home, our lives, for ways to make it happen. Starting an organization never seemed daunting to Dana; rather, it was natural. Now, from its humble beginnings, the organization she founded, Change for Change, reaches students and young professionals all over the country. This Reader's Digest's *"Everyday Hero" and* USA Today *All-American College Student explains how the whole thing came about.*

I was a sophomore at the University of Pennsylvania, packing up to move back to Minnesota for the summer, when I got the idea. As I looked around my emptying room, I saw the stadium cup into which I had pitched all those pennies from my pockets during the school year. It's amazing how much loose change a person can accumulate. It was too heavy to take on the plane with me, but I didn't want to just leave it behind either. That's when the light bulb came on and I had what I call an "aha!" moment. I was pretty sure I wasn't the only student facing the end-of-school-year-loose-change dilemma. Most of my friends had similar cups in their rooms. Loose change may not amount to much when it's yours, but in the collective it can amount to a big something, something really important to others. So, I thought about how meaningful an impact we could have if we put all of our change together and donated it to a charity. I started with my dorm, recruiting everyone I could to contribute their change. People loved the idea. I came up with the name "Change for Change," and it stuck.

From rounding up the change out of people's containers and couches, I then held door-to-door collections in the dorms, partnered with student groups to ask for their support in our collection drives, and even worked with local businesses. I remember the first time we held an official collection, two friends and I ended up with all these coins in a big plastic bag that was almost breaking at the seams. We dragged it down to Commerce Bank to their coin sorter, trying to guess how much we'd raised. We dumped all of those coins into the sorter, and sure enough, the machine spat out what it didn't want. It was right after spring break and there were pesos and other foreign coins flying back out of the machine: you could get a sense of where the students had been for their vacation. We collected about $1,000 in our first major effort and were thrilled.

Nowadays, we have lots of college campuses participating and have recently founded a chapter for young professionals in New York City. Each chapter raises funds how and when they choose. For instance, Amherst College hosts collections four times a year, with student athletes going door-to-door to collect change. Their efforts have certainly paid off, as they raised $4,000 last year. Our New York City chapter for young professionals donated $30,000 in its first year. It's still very important to me that our chapters support local charities while also rotating the causes they support, educating people about how many different charities there are. That way, Change for Change isn't about supporting just one good cause, but letting those who give learn about a multitude of good causes.

Since our first drive, we've built up a tool kit of additional support, everything from document templates, to an online homepage, to giving small grants to chapters to help with overhead expenses, to simply providing ongoing advice. Having a model and building up Change for Change's infrastructure is vital. You have to pick the right people—people who are excited to be involved, enthusiastic, who will have fun with it. I love what I'm doing, and the fun is in the challenge—building a Web site, incorporating, finding wonderful volunteers, developing materials, and coming up with fresh projects. Continuing to keep the organization creative has been one of the most intellectually stimulating parts about my work. And the stadium cup—in which I first collected my loose change—has remained a central component of our program. We provide customizable cups to all of our chapters, and they serve to remind young people not only to support causes they care about, but also of the good they can achieve when working with others. Sometimes people think young people don't care or can't make a difference. Change for Change shows that they can and they do. When young people get together and pool their efforts, small change can cause big changes.

Helping Bag the Plastic Plague

Getting Rebecca Hosking to contribute to this book took some doing. She lives behind the camera, shooting wildlife films for the BBC's Natural History Unit, and has no desire to be the one standing in front of it or, for that matter, giving interviews. But when the riveting documentary she made, Hawaii: Message in the Waves, *came out, she found herself in high demand from both the public and the press. Word had gotten out that she used what she learned on the islands to benefit first her entire Devonshire town of Modbury, and now, towns all over the world. She discovered how the plastic objects we use for almost everything end up in the oceans and on the shores of the world's most beautiful beaches, where they are killing wildlife. Rebecca's message is that we might just surprise ourselves by achieving important changes without much more than a belief that they need to happen and a willingness to collect the facts and make the case. I think you will be buoyed by her story.*

I was born and brought up in Modbury, a town—well, a village really—in Devon. My father runs an environmental farm: it's organic, the whole works. He farmed around wildlife, meaning that unlike many other farmers he never killed off badgers and foxes or birds of prey. Because of him, I pretty much had nature bludgeoned into me as a child! I was so immersed in plant and animal goings-on that, in school, my hand was always the one that shot up when the teacher asked a question about biology.

She started ignoring me and told my mother, "We have to give the other children a chance."

At fourteen, I picked up a camera and became absorbed in photographing the countryside. I learned everything I could about photography and decided that was how I wanted to spend my life. One day, when I was in my early twenties, the BBC arrived to film a documentary about my father's farm. I was between jobs and these men's lives—spent traveling the world—sounded so fantastically exotic to me that I made myself indispensable. I knew where all the animals were, all about the local landscape, and I knew cameras inside and out. I was the perfect assistant, from looking after their lenses to showing them around. They ended up agreeing to take me on permanently.

A few months later, I was employed to assist a BBC producer named Andrew Murray, a terrific man whom I've worked with ever since, and he suggested that I apply for the prestigious BBC Bursary. That was a two-year training scholarship that anyone wanting to break into the business would absolutely die for. He nagged me incessantly to try out for it, although I thought there was absolutely no chance I'd get it. I did apply, along with 7,000 other applicants, and when it got down to the final twenty, apart from me they were all boys! My joke, after I was chosen, was that the BBC must have decided to check the politically correct box, so that if I'd been a one-legged, lesbian, black, working-class single mother, they'd have picked me, too. But being the only "girl" was enough.

On that training course, I worked on Sir David Attenborough's world-renowned wildlife series, and I had the use of the most expensive equipment imaginable. When the two years were up and I graduated, I had to buy my own equipment and went into debt. My nickname for my camera today is "My House," because that's about what it cost me. It has taken years to pay it off. But I need it. I'm now one of only three women wildlife photographers in Britain, and one of only six in the world.

Out on the job, I began to be bothered by what we do. For example, we always show how beautiful nature is, and it is beautiful, but things aren't as perfect as they seem. There aren't that many real virgin areas left. Civilization is usually a lot closer, and the wilderness areas are usually far smaller than they appear on television. If you moved the camera a little to the right or left, for instance, you would see a lamppost, a road, sludge. I wanted to make something that addressed this disparity more honestly. With this in mind, our crew shot *Message in the Waves* in Hawaii. I'd become aware of the tremendous amount of plastic pollution worldwide. Every piece of plastic ever manufactured is still on our planet in some form. It doesn't break down for 500–1,000 years, no one exactly knows how long. In Hawaii, the pollution is particularly pronounced. The North Pacific currents work like a toilet bowl that never flushes; the water keeps going around and around because it's in the center and it acts like a vortex for the rubbish and debris from all the countries along the Pacific Rim and from America, Asia, and Russia. The whole lot just comes to rest there. We could have filmed in the Azores or along the North Cornish coast; there are countless places where this is an issue, but a larger audience would tune in if they imagined palm trees and paradise, and it was important to reach as many people as possible. At heart, it's a global film with the Hawaiian Islands representing a microcosm of the whole planet. In some areas of the oceans, for instance, the ratio of plastic to plankton is thirty to one, depending on the currents.

Tourists visit Hawaii and have no idea that the popular beaches are cleaned twice a week or twice a month. But, go to the beaches that are harder to reach and you're in for the shock of your life. On the south side of the big island of Hawaii, for instance, the plastic is four to six feet deep because the beach is only cleaned once a year. You're tromping over everything from brushes to ointment tubes to microwaves to CD players to cups to ink jet cartridges, children's toys, dummies, even alarm clocks. It may be solid or it may be particles, but it's all there. I'll never, ever buy a plastic coat hanger again; I saw so many of them. After the second day, the crew and I were so depressed, we had to walk away, sit down and think. Imagine: it isn't sand that you're walking on, it's particle plastic in colors of blues, greens, and reds. We all started recycling like mad.

The Midway Atoll, one of the Northwest Hawaiian Islands, was horrifying, although it's a protected wildlife reserve, the biggest marine reserve in the world. Here we found the biggest breeding ground in the world for the Laysan albatross. They're devoted parents that mate for life and groom each other so tenderly that you can't help relate to them. We watched them fly and were awed by how majestic they are in flight, but on the ground, they're pretty useless and have a very silly walk. These birds mistake colorful plastic bits floating on the sea as squid—their main food. They fly 1,000 miles out on an average hunting trip, swoop down, intake this plastic, and fly back to their chicks to unwittingly feed them this deadly meal. A turtle choked to death in front of us, plastic stuck all down his throat. We saw monk seals, called "dog that runs in rough water" by the Hawaiians, with their heads jammed into plastic tubs and plastic binding that was washing about. These endangered seals have such bad scarring from plastic that wildlife officials now identify each individual by their scars! Watching spinner dolphins play in the surf with plastic bags, thinking they were seaweed, was like watching a small child playing with a plastic bag and realizing how dangerous it was for them. Sometimes they get the bag wrapped around their blowhole and can't breathe, or they swallow it.

When I got home to the UK, I happened to go snorkeling one day and I was horrified at what I saw. There was plastic bag after plastic bag on the ocean floor here too! I kept diving down, picking up bags, sticking them in my bikini, and then holding more of them. When I came out of the water, I looked like the monster of the deep with all these plastic bits hanging off me. Everyone walking past stared! That afternoon, I was in a queue and noticed that no matter how tiny a purchase someone was making, the cashier would say, "Carrier bag?" and they'd say, "Yes, please!"

When I showed the film to my friend Adam, who runs a deli in the village, he was quite shocked. He said, "I don't want to stock plastic bags any more." Then another friend, Sue, who runs an art gallery, watched it. She was shocked as well. That's when I heard myself asking, "Could I show the film in your gallery?" When I saw her writing down a day, ten days away, in her gallery diary, I knew I had to get the job done: I wanted every trader in Modbury to see it and I wanted Modbury to be plastic bag free. There are forty-three shopkeepers in the village, and I got a list of all of them from the Chamber of Trade. I didn't pressure them. I simply went around, with a smile, saying, "Would you come and watch my film, please. There'll be wine and food. And I'm going to ask everyone to consider making Modbury the first town in Britain to be plastic bag free."

The night of the showing, I gave the first talk of my life, offered the facts and figures, and showed my film. People were appalled, especially when they saw the albatrosses' plight. At the end, we had a discussion. The smaller merchants were worried about the supermarkets and I had to reassure them that the supermarkets would look very bad if the small shops changed and the supermarkets, who always talked about how "green" they were, didn't. No other town in Britain had gone plastic bag free, but I'd found a wonderful Australian group called Planet Ark Foundation whose founder had provided me with all the information I needed to help people make the switch. His magic words were, "It can be done!" So, I explained the alternatives, like cornstarch bags and organic cloth bags. Then I called for a show of hands. To my amazement, they all raised their hands! I was taken aback. "Within a month, that's our challenge!" I said.

So, that's how Modbury became the first town in the UK to be plastic bag free (though I'm happy to say other towns are now following suit). My friend Adam used to give out 200 plastic bags a day; in the first week, he sold four cornstarch bags. The big supermarket gave away 1,000 plastic bags a day; in the first week, they sold 250 cornstarch bags. People now bring their own bags to the shops and everyone wins, including the oceans and wildlife. If anyone wishes to do the same thing, and I hope they will, I have put all the instructions on my Web site.

Hawaiian culture is incredibly respectful of the natural environment, and penalties for despoiling nature and wildlife were written into native law. What the West has done to despoil these once-pristine islands by "importing" its plastic waste via the ocean currents is absolutely awful. Hawaiians have a wonderful ethos called "Kuleana," which means that privilege—in this case, enjoyment of all that is beautiful in the natural world—comes with the responsibility—in this case of protecting it. To me, this term is something we should all work toward and try to achieve no matter where in the world we live.

ROBIN KEVAN (AKA ROB THE RUBBISH)

No Point in Grumbling!

Since his retirement a few years ago, Robin Kevan, a keen walker who loves being outdoors, is thoroughly enjoying his new "hobby." In fact, it not only gives him something constructive to do with part of his day, it has changed the face of the little Welsh town, Llanwrtyd Wells, where he lives with his wife Tina. What is it? Well, Rob has developed a keen interest in . . . garbage! Picking it up, that is. And he does it without a grumble. I relate to Rob, apart from the grumbling bit, because every weekend when I am at home, you can find me cleaning up after the construction workers who park their trucks along the road. As I scoop up the umpteenth empty liquor bottle, I have to wonder how the fourteen-story building they have erected doesn't wobble, for some of the workers couldn't have been that steady on their feet by day's end. Rob is a mega-version of me, someone who wants the world not only to be a beautiful place, but also to be a beautiful place to look at. Starting in Wales, he has now been as far afield as Mount Everest in pursuit of rubbish. The story of his litter-picker evolution perfectly illustrates how helping clean up even one patch of ground around us can make everyone's experience more enjoyable.

I've always loved being outdoors. I've definitely got a "thing" about wild open spaces. Where I live now is one of the prettiest places on earth, a beautiful rural village, officially the smallest "town" in Britain, with hills all around me. It's very wet here, but that's what makes it so green, the air so crisp. You might call this town "sleepy," but it's another story when people arrive here from all over the world for the "World Bog Snorkeling Championships!" Contestants put on a snorkel and have to swim underwater through a sixty-meter-long dark, cold, black, smelly peat bog pit, both ways, without surfacing. I've watched it many times.

I'm lucky in that where I was born and bred in the Yorkshire Dales, now called Cumbria, is one of Britain's great natural beauty spots, with an abundance of hills, rivers, and waterfalls. As a lad, I spent every free moment out in the fields, roaming wild and free. I loved to be out, particularly messing about along the riverbanks. Cities only appealed to me, the buzz of them, the bright lights, for a fleeting moment in my youth, but as I grew older I came to really appreciate the quiet and peace of the countryside. As an adult, I still walk a lot. Walking, especially walking up a mountain like Ben Nevis, Britain's tallest peak, makes me feel alive. I like the effort, I like to feel the wind and the rain hitting me; it touches my very soul. I think, "This is me! This is what I'm about." Walking in beautiful places is uplifting, mystic in a way, and everything in nature is beautiful really, no matter how different one place is from another.

When you are leading a busy life you can be oblivious to some things, but when you retire, you can slow down and notice things around you. I noticed that even in my beautiful town, people drop their crisp [potato chip] packets on the ground and toss their empty bottles and cans into the hedges. I live about 300 yards up a very rural road from our lovely town center and there's always litter staring up at me from behind the parked cars on the street. I regularly moaned to my wife about the mess and how irritating it was and how it took away from the impact of our little town, and one day she said "Well, why don't you stop grumbling and do something about it?"

It took a lot for me to start because I found it embarrassing. Only tramps are seen picking up things off the ground, cigarette butts and the like. So I decided to go out at dawn, when no one was about and pick all the litter up on our street. That day the road looked so much better that I felt very good about it. That's how it started: I was the Magic Fairy who cleaned everything up on our street before people left the house every day! Gradually I got more ambitious. I'm not obsessive, I've never been particularly tidy, but I could see that with just a little effort I could make a big difference, so I expanded my area, eventually cleaning up our main street and around a two-mile radius.

I don't usually run into people, but it occurred to me that if I did, I should be identified, so I got a yellow gillet, one of those workman's vests to wear. In our town, people are known by what they do. Our mailman is "Ken the Post," our milkman is "Hugh the Milk," our teacher is "Bryn the School," so my wife suggested I put "Rob the Rubbish" on the back of the vest. People came to know what I was doing after that. A woman who works in the Tourist Information Office told me that she had a litter stick that the council had provided but that was collecting dust out back of the office, so she gave it to me. No more bending down! I could now save my back and be three feet away from the rubbish I snagged. Nowadays, very nice people give me litter sticks, vests, even strong gloves.

I don't like rubbish, but I don't get angry when I see it. In fact, I have a curious and very positive relationship with it now. When I see something on the ground, I know that in a moment it's going to be gone and the natural beauty that's covered up by it will be revealed, and that makes me smile. When I remove "residual rubbish," nature starts to breathe again. The more you do, the better the whole place looks. The BBC's resident poet, Matt Harvey, called me a "topographic groomer" and I love that! Rubbish gets me going in a good way.

I have started going into schools. I've found a fun way to make my points about how important it is to clean up your own environment, how kids will inherit their patch of the Earth sooner than they think. I do that by putting ten crisp packets on the stage and asking the assembly if anyone would come and pick one up. Of course, no one wants to stand up in front of their friends and pick up rubbish, which is exactly how I felt when I started. The kids umm and ah and shuffle their feet, and then, eventually, someone does it, then another, and another. They all stand there, feeling a bit foolish, holding the rubbish. That's when I tell them to look into the packet they're holding. I put a five-pound note in one of the packets, and you should see their faces. Now everyone wishes they'd gone up! I tell them that you never know what you'll find, and in fact, I have found quite a bit of money in my years of cleaning up, along with other things, like a fully stocked first aid kit, fancy clothes, and even, to my great amusement and quite a puzzle, three sets of men's and women's underwear halfway up a mountain! Of course, the real reward for me is in knowing that I've restored beauty to a place.

As for my town, if I stopped cleaning up I can't say it wouldn't revert to its former grubby self; I just don't know. I don't know that the parts of Everest I cleaned up will or won't be litter strewn again either. But, I know that seeing someone clean up with enthusiasm is contagious. From my own neighbors to people I've met hiking, to the helpful villagers and Sherpas in the Himalayas—including one guest house owner whom I had a word with after seeing her slinging empty bottles over a virtual precipice—I know, because they've told me, that most of them are far more rubbish-conscious now.

Matt Harvey's poem about me has lines that sum it up:

. . . by picking up crisp packets, cling film and tin foil
Incongruous empties of Sprite and Drambui
He nurtures the flora and fauna and topsoil
And subtly recharges the Feng of its Shui.

Planning the U.S. Department of Peace

Representative Dennis Kucinich is not your run-of-the-mill congressman. The first thing you notice when you step through the huge oak-paneled doors into his office is what's on the walls. Like the man himself, there is no pomp, no pretension. In 1977, at age thirty-one, Kucinich was elected Mayor of Cleveland, the youngest person ever to lead a major American city. He was the 2003 recipient of the Gandhi Peace Award. And among other passions (and planks in his presidential bids), he advocates for a Department of Peace so as to make nonviolence an organizing principle in our society.

I asked Representative Kucinich to contribute an essay because he is so straightforward and unafraid to be open about his real agenda and beliefs. I find this refreshing when many politicians seem so fearful of deviating from a script carefully crafted to offend no one that they might as well be created from a single mold.

As far back as I can remember I knew I wanted to be in public service of one type or another. In the tenth grade, I envisioned myself running for national office. It was more intuition than anything. I just knew that's what I wanted to do. I ran for a seat for the first time when I was twenty-one and was on the City Council by the time I was twenty-three. Then

I went on to become the youngest mayor ever. I never had any doubts.

Public service always meant a lot to me. I read lots of biographies, and that opened up a whole world of experiences. I was very impressed that people dedicated their lives to a certain purpose, whether sports, religion, science, literature, or government, and had the ability to change things. That seemed worthwhile. My family believed in tolerance, in understanding, that no one was better than anyone else. They taught me compassion for anyone who is considered different than the rest. They instilled in me the belief that I could be one of those people who bring about change.

I was the first of seven children, and my parents never owned a home. By the time I was seventeen, we'd lived in twenty-one different places, just trying to find a place to stay, and on a couple of occasions we lived in our car. But that never made me feel separate from anyone else. Being the eldest, I had to be resourceful, self-reliant, strong. But there were times when I could have fallen through the cracks. Fortunately, there was always someone there to catch me. For example, when I was sixteen I felt school could offer me nothing more and that the real world was where I needed to be. One of my teachers was there to catch me and to insist, outright insist, that I stay in school. And I did.

Racism has always upset me very much, and I have always felt I could do something about it. When I was four, one of my friends was an African-American child named Dwight. One day we were playing outside and a passerby said something very crude to me about why I was playing with Dwight. When I went home, I asked my mother about it and she assured me that the person who made the remarks was wrong and that I had a lot in common with Dwight. Dwight became one of my best friends. This was my first real brush with racism.

Then, in Cleveland, in the mid-fifties, African Americans started moving into "white neighborhoods." People in those neighborhoods came out and protested. It was so unfair. I think people should be able to live where they want to live. I saw this personally and was very upset by it. After that, I paid greater attention to such discrimination. These were the early days of civil rights, and it never seemed fair that people should have to struggle this hard for equality. Seeing this, knowing people who were caught up in the struggle, made me realize that I needed to defend the principle of equality, that I could use the advantages I was lucky enough to have to stand up against bigotry, not only when it was directed against my friends like Dwight, but on a far larger scale. I realized that in public office I could actually make policy and set an example of fairness to all. Since I have been a congressman, I have had the opportunity to cosponsor numerous bills that would help protect or enhance the well-being and livelihood of people who sometimes get the short end of the stick. I've seized those opportunities with great joy by supporting, for example, school-based music education, Medicaid, a tax-cut repeal for the wealthy, assistance to those living in poverty, further research into an HIV vaccine, and religious tolerance. I've supported bills that focus directly on the needs and rights of minorities, such as condemning the existence of racially restrictive covenants in housing documents and recognizing the low presence of minorities in the financial services industry and in upper-level positions of management, and working to change that. And I've supported the goals and ideals of National Black HIV/AIDS Awareness Day and Anti-Slavery Day. I've also supported legislation that would honor several minority figures properly such as a posthumous pardon to Jack Johnson who went to jail, basically, for having a white girlfriend, Lena Horne for her outspoken opposition to racial and social injustice, Judge Constance Baker Motley for her courage, as both a woman and an African American in arguing key cases in front of the Supreme Court, and for Wangari Maathai for winning the Nobel Peace Prize for her tireless work promoting sustainable development, democracy, peace, and women's rights in Africa. Weighing in on these matters has meant the world to me.

If I have any advice for someone feeling unsure about what they can do in life, I would offer this: Each person who has the courage to follow his or her own dream and do it with joy, without compromise, will soon come in touch with great creative powers that may seem divinely inspired and that are in fact profoundly human.

From Mines to Vines

Heidi Kuhn founded Roots of Peace in 1997. The organization not only car-
ries on, but expands upon, the work of the late Princess Diana, removing land-
mines from fields in places as far flung as Afghanistan and Croatia, helping
plant crops like grapes and pineapples where once the fields were too dangerous
to plow, and advocating a ban on landmines. Her work with the soil, her own
roots (she was born in California just in time to absorb the peace and love mes-
sage of the sixties), the fact that she has four children of her own and likes to
be barefoot, in her kitchen, make Heidi Kuhn a true "Earth Mother." But the
photographs of her show a different side: a professional with a purpose, standing
with farmers at the grape harvest, discussing war and peace with Kofi Annan at
the United Nations, and presenting a pomegranate to President Hamid Karzai.
She fascinates me! Heidi didn't plan this path, but, as a young mother, Heidi
acted on her "women's intuition" and started filing news reports. She started in
Juneau and ended up in Moscow, where she captured some of the world's most
interesting and important news stories coming out of the Soviet Union. As she
tells the story, it was a matter of one thing simply leading to another.

I am a fifth-generation Marin County resident, born in San
Raphael. I am also a Roman Catholic, although I think religious ideals cross denominational barriers. Raphael is the patron
saint of healing. San Francisco, which is where I got the idea
to start the foundation, is named after St. Francis, whose words

"Dear God, make me an instrument of your peace" mean a great deal to me. I found myself saying similar words in 1988, when I was diagnosed with cervical cancer. There I was, in the incredible cold of the Alaskan tundra. I felt very alone. My husband was away on an extended business trip; I had babes-in-arms to care for, no friends in this out-of-the-way place, and my life was at risk from this insidious disease. I looked out at a fourth-of-July celebration and wondered if I would ever see another. Just before I went under anesthesia for the surgery, I prayed quietly, "Dear God, please grant me the gift of life. If you do, I promise I will do something special with it." I never forgot that pledge, and I still see every day as a gift, a chance to do something that represents the values I grew up with: love, peace, caring.

When the *Exxon Valdez* ran aground, I used contacts I had made with mainland news bureaus to file reports from the scene. Reporting seemed to suit me, and I enjoyed knowing that I was helping people in, say, New York, connect to people thousands of miles away. Soon I had an idea: why not go to the Soviet Union and try to cover the melting of the "ice curtain" between the U.S. and the Soviet government? At that time, no U.S. reporters were permitted access, and it was a bit of a scary prospect, entering the belly of the beast, knowing this was the superpower that had us all hiding under our desks in school, practicing how to survive a nuclear attack.

Everyone around me said, "No, don't go" and "It's impossible." Just getting a visa took six months. But you have to be partially deaf to work for social change, so I didn't listen. I wanted to tell the human story behind the thaw, and I was going to do my best to get in and get it. And things started to fall into place. My husband decided to take a leave to act as my cameraman, and a wonderful pediatric nurse we knew volunteered to look after the kids. Suddenly everyone was

empowering me! In December 1989, I found myself looking out of the plane window at the full moon, headed for
Moscow, wondering what I was doing. I didn't even have a
contract with a news agency; I just had an idea.

My grandmother used to say, "Coincidence is a miracle in
which God prefers to remain anonymous." As it turned out,
the Soviets denied U.S. reporters any access but had a special
relationship with Alaska. Because of that, I was the very first
reporter given the story of Andrei Sakharov's death, a worldwide exclusive that I raced across town to satellite feed to ABC
studios in New York. I proved that I could get the story and
that I could deliver it! One thing led to another. I found myself
not only able to report on peace, the warm and fuzzy "Yalta
to Malta" stories, but leading the first news crew into Vladivo-
stok and meeting every dignitary in the land. That stood me
in good stead for the charity work ahead of me when my life
changed again in 1997.

It was January and I was back in San Francisco. I had decided
to stop reporting, stop traveling, and be a stay-at-home mom
following the miraculous birth (my cervix had been removed
because of the cancer) of my son, Christian. People would often
ask if I could host events at my home, and I always said yes.
This time, the gathering was for a United Nations Association
touring the U.S. Lots of my neighbors are vintners. I thought
"why not?" so I called up Francis Ford Coppola and asked if
he would supply the wine. He agreed right off the bat. Then
I asked my childhood friend, Mike, who is a concert pianist, if
he'd play, and he said he would.

All this was just weeks after Princess Diana's death, and her
work to get landmines banned was on my mind; it was so smart,
so right. On the night of the event, Jerry White, the man who
had escorted Princess Diana through Bosnia, was in my living
room. He is an Irishman, a Catholic like me, and very inspiring.

At some point, he simply bent down and pulled off his artificial leg. He told me that he had stepped on a landmine while walking in the Golan Heights. He remembers lying there, yelling, "My leg. My leg. My god, where's my leg?!"

It was a very moving evening. There was Jerry, there was my friend Mike playing "Candle in the Wind," and I felt as if I were part of a wonderful watercolor painting. I wondered how I could not have known about the devastation wrought by landmines, all the work that was needed to get rid of them. Listening to the speakers, talking to the guests who had come from all over the world, I felt as if generational wisdom, the calls for compassion and peace, were echoing back from my childhood in the sixties. I wanted the earth and her people to be thought of as sacred, for all hatred to be replaced with love. It was as if I could feel the blood of all those who are unjustly hurt being washed away by the donated wine. I knew what I wanted to do. I wanted to help carry on Princess Diana's work. We lifted our glasses for the toast, and I heard myself saying, "May the world go from mines to vines." You could have heard a pin drop.

Since then, I have walked the minefields of the world in the name of peace. I meet with the farmers, relate to their families as a mother and as a Christian who cares about tolerance, interfaith love, and diplomacy. That is something everyone I've met has seemed to respect and understand. There is nothing more important to me than knowing that the sum total of landmine production has dropped, that families who depended on farming have been able to return to the soil, and that there is more peace in the land than there was before Roots of Peace started.

We have removed over 100,000 landmines and unexploded ordnance and trained some 10,000 Afghan farmers to grow clusters of grapes instead of sidestepping clusters of bombs.

We have raised funds to help in Croatia, Bosnia-Herzegovena, Angola, and Afghanistan. And perhaps the most wonderful recognition of this work is the Roots of Peace garden in New York City, donated to us by the United Nations.

On its wall is a plaque that reads:

"They shall beat their swords into ploughshares, and their spears into pruning-hooks; nation shall not lift up sword against nation, neither shall they learn war any more."

To me, the mines are the swords and the vines are the ploughshares, and our work to build bridges of peace will go on until love defeats hate.

The Future Is Fantastic!

PBS called him one of the sixteen "revolutionaries who made America." A list, mind you, that encompassed inventors of the past 200 years. He has received the National Medal of Technology, the nation's highest technical honor; has been inducted into the National Inventor's Hall of Fame by the U.S. Patent Office; was named MIT's Inventor of the Year; and was ranked by Forbes magazine as "the rightful heir to Thomas Edison." A mere five plucked from his endless list of accomplishments.

Ray Kurzweil is a genius in the field of artificial intelligence. He is responsible for more "firsts" than any other living inventor, including the first text-to-speech synthesizer, created for the blind and reading-impaired. In the 1970s, at Stevie Wonder's urging, he developed a computer that could so realistically recreate the musical response of the grand piano and other orchestral instruments that musicians were unable to distinguish its sounds from that of the actual instruments. Among Ray's many fascinating books are The Singularity Is Near: When Humans Transcend Biology, *a New York Times bestseller, and* The Age of Spiritual Machines: When Computers Exceed Human Intelligence. *In them, we read of how a once-futuristic vision of a machine-dominated world is only twenty or so years away and isn't as frightening as we might think. Ray Kurzweil's latest ventures include FATKAT, an artificial intelligent financial analyst. He belongs in this book because while few people can match the power of his brain, his enthusiasm for what the future holds can be contagious.*

116

was always confident that I would be an inventor. Even at five, I felt you could create almost magical effects with inventions. All around me, other kids were wondering what they "would be," but I knew what I was going to be. When I was eight, I built a mechanical puppet theater with a control station from which I could move the sun and moon in and out, move stars and clouds, and characters on and off stage. It was my first foray into virtual reality. When I was sixteen, I appeared on a TV show called *I've Got a Secret*, hosted by Steve Allen. I walked onstage and played a piece of music on the piano, then told Steve that my secret was that I had built my own computer. Steve was puzzled and asked, "What has that got to do with the piece you just played?" I told him that the computer had composed it. Building that computer was a high school project and my first venture into teaching computers to recognize abstract patterns, the capability that dominates human thinking. That project won first prize at the International Science Fair and an audience with President Lyndon Johnson at the White House awards ceremony.

After that, I went on to study computer science and literature at MIT. I quickly realized that timing was critical to success as an inventor. Ninety percent of inventions fail not because the inventor can't get them to work, but rather because the timing is wrong; not all the factors needed are in place. Inspired by this, I became an ardent student of technology trends. I tracked where technology would be at various points in time and built mathematical models of my findings. From this I discovered that technology is growing exponentially, as opposed to the conventionally held view that its growth is linear. For instance, it took us half a century to adopt the telephone, our first virtual reality technology, but only about eight years to adopt cell phones.

Due to its exponential growth pattern, information technology is doubling its power every year, which means that we will achieve the capability of human intelligence in a machine by 2029. It will then soar past our current understanding because of the continuing acceleration of information-based technologies and the ability of machines to not only process information and make decisions based upon it, but to instantly share their knowledge with each other. When the time comes that computers are far smarter than human beings, a moment I call the Singularity (a metaphor borrowed from physics referring to an event horizon beyond a black hole and past which we cannot readily see), it won't be from an invasion of machines from outer space, but from within, from technology that we have created. The impact of this will be so deep that human life will be irreversibly changed.

Although it's hard to grasp how different our world will be, we shouldn't be scared of the coming transition: it will be a revolution that radically enhances rather than destroys human life. We'll be able to access and master so much more information at such an incredible speed, and the technology to use it will make today's pocket computers seem very primitive. Even before the Singularity, intelligent nanobots (robots smaller than human blood cells) will be deeply integrated into our bodies, our brains, and our environment. They'll be injected into our bloodstream and interact intimately with our own biological systems, detect problems, slow down the aging process, turn genes on and off, and help us keep our bodies healthy. We're already reverse-engineering the human brain, simulating the functioning of many regions of the brain including the cerebellum, and modeling how our neurons work. In about twenty years, nanobots swimming in our brain capillaries will increase our brainpower substantially as they communicate with our biological neurons, as well as with each other over a wireless local network and with the Internet. Similarly, nanobots in the environment will be capable of reversing environmental degradation, in particular removing carbon dioxide from the air. They also have the means to revolutionize renewable energy by providing efficient nano solar cells, for example, and nanoscale fuel cells to store the energy. I find all of this very exciting; therefore, I take care of my health using today's knowledge, being careful to eat lots of vegetables and fruits, to drink green tea and alkaline water and take supplements to "reprogram" my biochemistry. I don't tailgate! I want to live long enough to enjoy the benefits of technology that can increase our life spans and eventually give us effective immortality.

The future will be remarkable indeed. By 2029, we'll see the full maturity of these trends. We have to appreciate how many generations of technology it took to get us there. The first step took tens of thousands of years: stone tools, fire, the wheel. Since then, we've always used the latest generation of technology to create the next generation. The first computers were designed with pen and paper, now we use computers. We've had a continual acceleration of this process right through to nanobots! They'll first be used for medical and health applications, cleaning up the environment, and providing powerful solar panels and widely distributed, decentralized fuel cells. These technologies are very democratizing. Technology development means that knowledge sharing isn't limited to big corporations, but accessible to anyone, anywhere in the world. For instance, because of the Internet, kids in, say, Pakistan and Nigeria, have access to the highest quality education. That is happening in villages where students gather around a computer and take courses from my old alma mater, MIT, for free using MIT's "Open CourseWare" program. Virtual reality technology is improving to the point where within a decade there won't be a discernible difference between being there or not; cell phone calls will soon be prosaic, as people will "meet" in various virtual environments instead. Within a quarter century, by interacting with our biological neurons we'll be able to experience full-immersion virtual reality from within the nervous system. The nanobots will shut down the signals coming from your real senses and replace them with the signals your brain would be receiving if you were in that virtual environment. You can visit these virtual surroundings with other people and have any kind of experience involving all of the senses. "Experience beamers," as I call them, will be able to put their whole flow of sensory experiences out there on the Internet so that others can plug in and feel what it's like to be someone else. But most importantly, it will be a huge expansion of human intelligence through direct merger with this technology. These technologies hold both our promise and our peril, so we must have the will to apply them to the right problems.

The thrill for an inventor is making a difference in people's lives. Hearing from blind or dyslexic people who say that my reading technology—which translates print into speech— enabled them to get an education or do their jobs, is the real reward. It's also exciting when musicians and musical groups send me their albums with messages indicating how the Kurzweil music technology (by which a world of sound is available to them on a computer) enabled them to create new sounds.

As far as I'm concerned, failure is just success deferred. For example, consider what a "failure" Thomas Edison was. He tried over 1,000 filaments and none of them worked. Until, that is, he found one that did. We don't remember all of those "failures." People fail only because they declare themselves to have failed.

From Pom-Poms to Playbook

The photographs of Bonnie-Jill Laflin that you see if you click onto her Web site are jaw-droppers. Sometimes wearing little more than a cowboy hat and a pair of tight denim shorts, her pearly white teeth visible behind a dazzling smile, Bonnie-Jill is the quintessential all-American pin-up (a fact not lost on the troops she has entertained on her USO tour of Iraq). It would surprise no one that this model and dancer guest-starred on Baywatch, *has been named one of* Maxim's *"Hot 100 Women," and was a cheerleader with the Golden State Warriors, the San Francisco 49ers, and the Dallas Cowboys (2,500 girls auditioned for that job). What is likely to surprise anyone is that she is the first female scout for the NBA.*

I met Bonnie-Jill when she posed for PETA's poster against the rodeo that reads: "No one likes an eight-second ride." And while men in sports have discovered that behind those drop-dead looks there is a woman who knows the teams, the players, and the stats, I discovered a kindhearted person who once stopped her car to scoop up a little dog that was being beaten by two youths and has protested the bullfight. All that aside, for anyone who has fought for his or her dream, Bonnie-Jill Laflin is worth listening to.

I have always loved sports. My father was a policeman who moonlighted as a bodyguard for sports figures like Jerry Buss, the owner of the Lakers, so I've been around men in sports my whole life. I looked up to them as a kid; they were like my big brothers. Everyone in my family, from my dad, with his various season tickets, to my uncle to my mother, was an avid sports fan. My dad took me to my first game when I was two years old. After that, we went to all the football games, baseball games, and basketball games. I remember people would see me sitting in the stands and would say, "Oh, get the little girl some Crackerjacks or some of that candy," and I would think, "No! I don't want that. I want to watch. I want to know how fast that guy ran the forty." I soaked up stats like a sponge. When the paper was delivered in the morning, another kid might have grabbed the funnies, but I grabbed the sports pages. I loved playing sports and talking sports and watching sports, and I knew I always wanted to be in sports.

Sports is very much a man's world. It is now, and was even more so a couple of decades ago. I never dreamed I could break into it professionally. Fortunately, I loved to dance. I knew my dancing could get me into cheerleading, and then I'd have the best seats in the house! When I was eighteen, I started cheerleading for the NBA and then the NFL. My most prized possession is the Super Bowl XXIX ring I won when I was cheering for the 49ers. Of course, I also prize my three rings from the Lakers' wins and wear one or two of them on most days. In one way, cheerleading opened some doors because I got to know so many more people in sports, and that networking helped when I worked my way into sports broadcasting. In another, it has been a hindrance, leading to the "Oh, she was a cheerleader" kind of attitude that allows people who don't know me to dismiss me.

During my broadcasting career, each interview was a hill to climb. Sports broadcasting is a man's world too, and people can try to lock you out. A lot of men don't think women should be on the airways talking about "their" game. I would have a hard time even getting an interview for a job. They would think

"What can this pretty little miss possibly know?" or "We don't have time for this kind of girl." But that only made me hungrier to succeed, that much more determined to break the barrier. Once my agent was able to get me meetings and I could sit down with the people at the different networks, they were taken aback by how much I knew. As I spoke I could see their eyes open and their minds going "Wait a sec. . . ." I started getting jobs as a correspondent at ESPN and CBS doing sports news.

But even then, I ran into difficulties. Some men, older men particularly, think of me in a certain way; it's hard for them not to because of tradition and what they have been used to their whole lives. Some guys make certain settings really uncomfortable, and they won't help you in the way they would help a man. They don't want to get to know you, and they won't treat you as a human being, just as a "girl." I have done a lot of different things, including study hard and start a sports clothing business, but if they look me up online and see those sexy photos, they think that's the sum total of me. Jerry Buss has been like a father to me; his family is like my own. But even he'll admit that he had to think hard about hiring a woman; he'll tell you straight that he was a male chauvinist. I understand that. But he was good about it. He sat me down and grilled me on football and basketball and, when he saw that I knew my stuff, he decided I deserved a chance to succeed.

Because of Jerry's decision, I'm the first female scout in the NBA, and that's exciting. When I'm out, I might be on the lookout to fill a particular spot—a power forward or a point guard, maybe—or looking at everybody as potential prospects. I have an edge in a way, because women can sometimes spot things men aren't programmed to notice. We can sometimes pick up on a person's chemistry. Maybe a coach has told me he's looking for a quick and speedy guy or maybe we need a taller guard, but first of all you have to have a player who will be "coachable," not someone who's arrogant and won't listen. I look for someone who can keep the team spirit up even when things go wrong, someone who meshes well with the others, because this isn't a one-man sport. If a player has a good attitude, that can make all the difference in a game. After that, you look for the fundamental skills; they have to be smart or they can't learn the playbook.

The whole management at the Lakers is terrific and supportive. They've taken me under their wing and they treat me with respect. At first I thought I would just sit there and be ignored, so it was a really big moment for me the first time I was asked for my opinion, the first time when I heard the magic words, "What do you think?" It can be tough when I'm on the road working with other offices in the League, because I have to prove myself at every step. If I'm in a meeting and they ask me something and I don't know, I'm done! At those times, Jerry's words ring in my head: "No matter what people think, it doesn't matter. Prove them wrong!"

High school girls and college women get in touch with me all the time to ask me how to break down the barriers and break into sports. I tell them that everyone in the world has to work to gain respect, and I'm still working on it. I haven't hit my best yet, but I'm working at it. You need to get a start and struggle on and study the game. Become an intern, find a toehold, and keep going. There's a lot to that slogan from the *Rocky Horror Picture Show*, "Don't dream it, be it!"

When Life Calls,
Be Packed and Ready!

Nobel Peace Prize–winning author Wangari Maathi campaigns to cancel the debts of the poorest countries in Africa and has been imprisoned and beaten for protesting against land grabbing and what she calls the "theft" of public forests. She has served on the United Nations Commission for Global Governance and the Commission on the Future. She is also the founder of the Green Belt Movement, a grassroots organization that improves the quality of life for African women and the environment through tree-planting programs.

Born into a farming family in the highlands of Mount Kenya in 1940, Professor Maathai was the first woman in East and Central Africa to earn a doctoral degree (pursuing studies in Pennsylvania, Kansas, and in Germany as well as in Africa) before becoming the first woman to hold a chair position at the University of Nairobi. In 2002, she was elected to Kenya's Parliament, carrying 98 percent of the vote, and later was appointed assistant minister for the environment. Forbes and Time magazines have both named her as one of the 100 most influential people in the world. She belongs in this book for her achievements, which are too many to list here, and for her beacon-like energy and determination.

The sort of life I live doesn't come with a blueprint. And I must be honest, I haven't examined it critically to see why I did this, or then why that happened. Nevertheless, I would

125

say it is very important to prepare yourself psychologically, health-wise, and so on, so that you are ready to take advantage of opportunities when they come. I recently heard somebody say that what we call luck is simply when opportunity meets preparedness. I think there's a lot of sense in that. When you're young, it's difficult to have this preparedness, though the challenges are there. The challenge of leaving home, of going to school, for me at a time when there was insecurity in the country. Then later on, the challenge of staying in school because there are so many temptations that make it difficult for a girl to stay focused and not to be distracted, especially when you are in a society where not every girl is being persuaded to go to school. And then of course, the challenge of leaving home permanently and not knowing what lies ahead and having to trust that everything will be okay. These sort of situations force you to trust in yourself, trust in a greater energy, and trust in the people who are guiding you. Quite often, these guides turn out to be good friends, which is fortunate because it would be impossible to do everything without the people that you meet on the way. Life is a journey that you walk with other people. If you are lucky, they become positive influences and help you to have a positive experience. If you are unlucky or you end up in the wrong company, then of course they can contribute toward your negative experiences in life. I can say I was sometimes lucky.

None of us can see what lies ahead, and because of this we tend to look at the future with fear. When you have confidence and trust it's much easier to deal with this fear. And also, when you imagine the possibilities of what could come out of what you are trying to do, then that becomes a source of inspiration and encouragement.

This way of thinking may come naturally to some, but most of us need to teach ourselves along the way. That is why, largely, this sort of confidence doesn't happen in our earlier years. During those years we're being guided by our parents, our teachers, and it's only when we get out of school and face the world that we begin to be challenged. It's from facing challenges, big ones or small ones, that trust and self-assurance builds.

Of course, there are times when you're not very sure how things are going to turn out, and when they turn out well, you say, "Thank God." I definitely do believe in a higher power, in a higher energy that is sometimes impossible to explain. We have given it many names in different communities. Whether we call it God or the angels or whatever, it is what guides us through seemingly impossible times. I've faced too many obstacles to list here, but I think I survived the moments of difficulties because of a strong commitment not only to God, but also to a need to succeed. Partly because I had people ahead of me whom I'd looked up to and whom I did not like to disappoint. And partly because there were people behind me, whom I did not want to disappoint. I hoped to give them strength by keeping strong, by keeping on, by not giving up. I think those are the forces that sometimes give us energy that we don't necessarily understand.

Conviction, vigilance, preparedness, confidence, imagination, these are some of the traits that bring victory, and victory brings great joy. As do your accomplishments, especially accomplishments that are likely to outlive you. These are accomplishments that will testify to your belief and your faith long after you're gone. If you believe that you have improved the situation for the better, this makes you feel that life is worth living. It is good to remember that quite often we are not challenged by major things, we are challenged by ordinary things in our ordinary life. Meeting these challenges is no less worthy or meaningful than meeting the monumental ones. The most vital thing is to meet any challenge with determination and joy.

Throwing Out a Lifeline

When I was a little girl, I often traveled through the Middle East. To me, all those women in "purdah" (literally meaning a "curtain" that excludes them from the world), a tiny cloth mesh window in their burqas allowing them to see the world like blinkered horses, were simply a part of the landscape. I am sorry to say that I didn't think of them as consequential at all, and that's how it is supposed to be. Even male imbeciles are full participants in society's business, whereas the cleverest woman counts only as half a person who must obey him in all things. She can never walk unaccompanied and, in many places, is forbidden to attend school or to work. My shame at so many years of not "seeing" these covered women may contribute to my attraction to Lily Mazahery's work. Lily is not only making them visible but also giving them a voice in the courts. Sometimes she saves their lives, which are often in danger for reasons that defy humanity.

Lily's whole country, Iran, became a happily forgotten place to her when she fled it as a child during the revolution. But now it has returned to her consciousness with a bang, and she is showing just how strong and useful a liberated woman can be.

Since the revolution in Iran, it is perfectly legal to stone a woman to death under Sharia, the Islamic laws put in place by the religious bodies that seized control of the country. It happens this way: a woman is forcefully pushed into a pit dug in the earth. Her hands are tied behind her back. Dirt is thrown into the pit until she is buried up to her chest. People then stamp on the earth to tamp it down and make her escape impossible. Her own relatives often throw the first stones, which, by law, must not be big enough to kill her outright. Then everyone joins in until she is finished. Can you imagine it? Women are killed in this way for the "crime" of adultery. An adulterous man, on the other hand, will get only a public lashing. Men are also allowed to take multiple young women, children really, as their wives, a form of sanctioned serial adultery and polygamy.

Women can also be stoned to death for flirting, for being caught holding hands with a man who is not related to them even when they are single, and for being raped. Yes, raped! The word for rape, "zena," is the same as that for debauchery and debauchery is a crime punishable by death under Sharia.

I was born in Teheran and was about five years old when the revolution came. I remember the chaos, shouting, flags burning, and our family life being turned upside down. I was upstairs studying at a little desk in a quiet room with floor to ceiling windows, when someone threw a Molotov cocktail into the house. Then another. Everything went up in flames and we ran out, my mother carrying my newborn baby brother in her arms. The worst blow of all was when my father, who worked for the government, had to leave us, to leave the country. It was six long years before we could join him.

We were reunited with my father the minute we stepped off the plane at JFK. I was jubilant. I didn't want to think about Iran ever again. I associated my life there with trauma, with loneliness, with missing my dad, with fear. Now I was going to be an all-American girl, speak English, play with American girls, go to an American school. A month after we were reunited with my father in the United States, my maternal grandmother, the closest remaining relative in Iran, died, and a door closed on that world for me. I told myself I would never speak a word of Farsi again. I was going to be an American teen! And that's what I became, completely.

My father was a civil engineer. When I was about fourteen, he took me, very proudly, to the opening of a law school he had designed. It was a beautiful day and during the opening ceremony I made up my mind to become an attorney. That was my path.

Around that time I met an Iranian girl I will call "Leila" who came from a broken home, and my own parents pretty much adopted her as their own. We were close until I went to college and then we lost touch. I found out that Leila had become pregnant at the age of seventeen, married the older man responsible, and moved to Kansas. Then, in my first year of law school, she called to say he was taking her back to Iran. She didn't want to go but she had no choice. I found it unbelievable, but I put it out of my mind and wished her well.

I really did live the American dream. I graduated top of my class and was recruited by one of the best law firms in the world, Jones Bay. This meant limousines, an expense account, big money, the works; all you strive for to be successful. Sitting in my office one day, I heard from my friend again. Leila now had two children. Her husband was abusive to her and she had found out that he not only had another wife in the United States, but the first wife was moving to Iran to live under the same roof with them. Leila was horrified and desperate to come back to America. What could I do but try to help her?

I worked around the clock. By getting on the Internet and searching, I found many people with connections in Iran, with legal training, even college groups of expatriates who were willing to help. Finally, we had enough of a legal leg to stand on to allow Leila to get a divorce hearing. If she could be freed from her husband's control, she could leave. I was so happy for her. But, when she went before the court, the judge asked her if it was "that time of the month." Flummoxed, Leila admitted that it was. That is when we found out that women are considered incompetent to make decisions at those times and Leila's divorce was flatly denied. Leila paid a man to help her flee to Turkey with the children, but September 11, 2001, was only days away. Even a world away, everything would change when those planes flew into the World Trade Center. Leila ended up unable to cross the border. Her husband found her, kidnapped her, and took her back. She's still there today.

This experience shook me from my ivory tower. I had family myself. I had legal training. I had a deliberately severed link to a country where my friend and other women like her were treated like things, where human rights did not extend to them. And the more I studied, the more I realized that this was not always the case in Iran. Going back to the days of Cyrus the Great, the Persian Empire, human rights were an important part of the development of the country. Now, reading the new penal code introduced since the revolution, those rights have been stripped away to the extent that a woman has no inheritance rights, no right to custody of her own children, and can be stoned to death for falling in love, for a wide array of ridiculous and harmless things labeled "acts incompatible with chastity"!

Perhaps the last straw was learning of a sixteen-year-old girl who was hanged in public for riding in a car with a boy. I couldn't sit still after that, so I started to contact jurists in Iran, and the more people I talked to, the more I learned. I made contacts with other lawyers in the United States who wanted to help. That's how I ended up founding the Legal Rights Institute, a nongovernmental organization, an international support network really, to fight for the rights of women and children in my former home.

One of our first cases involved a woman who was gang-raped while she tried to defend her niece. When she went to the police for help she was arrested and ended up sentenced to death because she had had physical contact with the men! Such women usually have no chance, the courts are kangaroo courts and there is no freedom of the press. Through persistence and determination and with much help from people on the ground in Iran, we were able to get her sentence commuted.

Another effort is our "One Million Signature Campaign," for which I started a petition drive in the United States, to collect a million signatures asking the government of Iran to treat men and women equally. We work with human rights lawyers who travel in and out of Iran, helping get women out of jail, getting them representation in the courts, trying to save their lives. We send little things to the women in jail, too, that make them realize that someone out there cares about them, is working to free them: flowers, photos, and once, even painting supplies for a prisoner named Delara Darabi. So many women commit suicide, their despair is so great; we try to ease that sorrow, give them hope, and bring a smile to their lips. There is not a day that I don't cry over a case I know about, one woman or another. Yet there we are, 9,000 miles away, digging for information, making contacts nearer to her, looking for legal remedies, trying to help her.

It was one thing for me to put in insane hours representing a *Fortune* 100 company. It is another to put in double those hours and save a life. To see the impact of my work on one living being's life, even if I never meet that person face to face, even if she will never know me, is such a reward for me. To know she will see her children again, nothing can compare with that.

I know it's odd that it's a Chinese, not an Iranian, proverb, but I keep this proverb on my desk. It reads, "When a finger points at the moon, the imbecile looks at the finger." I like to think that in my small way I am the pointing finger to a much larger concept than one case here, one case there, but to the eventual liberation of women in Iran. That proverb keeps me motivated. The goal is all that matters, and my goal is to see women free enough to dance on the moon.

All You Need Is Passion, Passion Is All You Need

When I was in my teens, the girls from my dorm and I used to take a battery-operated record player out onto the hill behind our convent boarding school and listen to our cherished RPMs. Among them was "Thank You, Girl" by the Beatles. It was so badly warped by the Indian sun (our school was in the Himalayas) that we had to tie increasingly heavy weights to the stylo to keep it from skipping and hiccoughing. I told Paul about that recently because he and Chrissy Hynde had been serenading Paul's daughter, Stella, with that song after her spring fashion show in Paris, a perfect tribute for her.

The thing about Paul is that he's down to earth. In the early sixties, when I started the All-India Beatles fan club, a hoity-toity nun who found out about it hauled me in front of school assembly and said, "Do you realize that these boys are from the slums of Liverpool?" What I knew then is that they were "working class," and what I know now is that Paul has never turned his back on those roots. Class meant a lot some sixty years ago, and Paul triumphed by touching millions of hearts, crossing that ridiculous barrier and holding his hand out, even today, to help others to do the same. That's the story that belongs in this book.

I used to listen to the radio a lot when I was a kid. The music was mostly from my dad's generation, Fred Astaire, whatever. Later, my dad, who was an amateur musician, pointed out the sound of the bass to me. He said, "Listen! Do you hear that booming noise? That's the bass." I listened and it intrigued me. That's when I decided to find out how music was done.

My dad gave me a trumpet for a birthday present, but I really wanted to sing and you can't sing if you've got something in your mouth, so I asked him if he'd mind very much if I traded it for a guitar. He said all right, so off I went, down to the music shop in town, Rushworth and Draper it was called. I got a cheap, simple guitar called a Zenith. I love it, I still have it. I never took lessons but I had a guitar book that I used to teach myself how to play. There were little dots to help you learn where to put your fingers so you could make chords. I learned the chords G, G7, C, and F. When I got really going, I went on to learn rock and roll, copying songs like Eddie Cochran's "20 Flight Rock," about a girl dancing with you on a Saturday night to a "record machine," that kind of stuff. Then a film came out in 1956 starring Britain's sex symbol, Jayne Mansfield, about a girl who wants to be a singing star. It was a great influence because this film did rock and roll proud. It was in color on a wide screen, and it treated rock and roll with respect. It had Fats Domino in it, Little Richard, Gene Vincent, and Eddie Cochran. Jayne Mansfield wasn't bad either!

The first song I ever wrote was called "I Lost My Little Girl." I can't remember now why I wrote it. I used to play with my mates at first. Later, John and I got together. He asked me if I'd like to play with his group, The Quarrymen, and when I said I would he put me on lead guitar. It was a disaster. I just froze up and completely botched the whole thing. It was so awful I made a determination never to play lead again, and I only recently got the courage to! I played lead guitar on some recordings in the sixties, but never live until recently. If you play lead, you have a big responsibility. I switched to bass guitar!

I remember the first applause we got. We were playing at the Wilson Hall in Liverpool, this large church hall kind of place, a long room, lots of people had come to listen to the bands. We weren't the only band on that night; there were a few more than us. We didn't do badly. It was gratifying to have rehearsed, practice we called it, until you had it right. John and I would try out songs on my dad. My dad always had a funny take on things. We played him "She Loves You," and my dad said, "Son, it's very nice." He really did like it. "But," he said, "there's enough of these Americanisms around these days, can't you sing 'Yes, yes, yes' instead of 'Yeah, yeah, yeah?'" "No, dad!"

If you have talent, you can teach yourself. We all did. If you have a big enough passion for music you can always beg or borrow (don't steal!) an instrument from somewhere and get a basic chord book, if you are learning the guitar, it's all the tuition you need. You can do a lot with that. Listen to a record, take the words down, and practice. My bedroom was my practice room. If you teach yourself, you are less likely to be doing what everyone else does. Your personal taste will lead you. Lots of people who can't play the piano but who fool around on it come across something just plonking about. Someone will ask, "What chord is that?" And they'll say, "I don't know, but it sounds good. Let's make a song!" That's how we did it. No Beatle ever had a lesson, and almost none of the people in my field can even read music. If you put a sheet of music in front of me to this day, it doesn't mean anything to me. I don't associate the dots on the page with what I do!

I think music is a magical thing and learning it teaches you a lot about self-discovery. You can learn from your mistakes, and your passion for it can actually lead you down a path no one could have taken you to. Often John and I would be mucking about and we'd discover a chord quite by accident and build a whole song around it. It's very exciting to do that. The opening track on my new record has a bit like that in it. I don't know anything about the mandolin other than it's a lovely instrument. It's not like a guitar, it's tuned like a violin, and so I had to go back to the basics like when I was sixteen again to learn to play it. I found a couple of chords I liked. One was off the Richter scale, probably the most interesting chord I've ever found. I've put that in this new song about dancing. When I was putting it together last Christmas, my little daughter Beatrice kept running into the room and dancing to it every time. I fell in love with that song because of her. That's two passions in one, music and this lovely little girl.

Creating with a Conscience

I am deeply fond of Stella McCartney because she is her mother's girl, kind and caring. Now with children of her own, she imbues them with the values she inherited from the woman known as "Angel for the Animals," Linda McCartney. But Stella is also a powerful force in the world of fashion. She may have been born with a silver spoon in her mouth, but she has made her own way, rising to the pinnacle of the fashion industry. What makes her clothes special is not only her relaxed, natural style but her steadfast, ethical decision never to use fur or leather in anything she designs, even shoes. In 1997, just two years out of school, she was appointed creative director of Chloe. Karl Lagerfeld greeted her appointment to his old position as an affront to his trademark leather pants and his old-fashioned focus on fur. Snarled Karl, "Let's hope she's as gifted as her father."

"Unstoppable Stella," as she's known in the fashion business, has proved that she is indeed. In 2001, she launched her own label under her name and the applause hasn't quieted yet. Her clothes are snatched up by those in the public spotlight, from Scarlett Johansson and Kate Moss to Gwyneth Paltrow and Madonna, who commissioned Stella to design some of her costumes for her Reinvention Tour. And Stella has not only won a VH1/Vogue Designer of the Year Award, but the line of clothing she designed for European mega-store H&M sold out on the day it hit the racks. Similar gob-smackingly successful collaborations have followed. The world loves Stella McCartney designs, and I suspect you will love Stella.

It's funny really, but I've been drawn to fashion from the moment, when I was about three years old, that a pair of glittery platform boots mesmerized me from my mother's wardrobe. I remember sitting on the floor, staring at them in awe. I'm sure I tried to put them on! I designed my very first piece of clothing, a jacket, when I was twelve. It was an eighties-style, slightly blouson jacket; the sort of dirty pink I'm known for on the inside and a dark navy, touching on black, on the outside. I was really happy with the result, and the jacket felt good to wear. In fact, I still think of it fondly. I can't remember if anyone commented on what I had done, but no one threw rotten tomatoes at me when I wore it.

When I was thirteen-ish and at school in England, it came time to determine a course of study. Would I be more likely to end up selling mutual funds, dissecting beetles, or painting frescos? Should I choose courses in the arts and design or business? I was really afraid of getting to be thirty and not knowing what I wanted to do, so I decided then to become a designer. Once I set my mind, I stuck to it. When I was fifteen, I managed to get an internship with Christian Lacroix in Paris. That was really amazing! He was preparing his first couture show, and there I was, mostly making coffee, counting buttons, threading shoelaces, but I was in the thick of it. It was ridiculously glamorous. And I was able to attend lots of incredible shows. The whole thing was a life-changing experience. Later, after my studies at St. Martins College of Art & Design, I was asked to come back to Paris. Luckily, I already had the confidence that is inevitable for a person to gain when you've worked at that level of Parisian couture, if only as an intern.

I grew up with two of the most famous ethical vegetarians in the world. Both my parents have been active with PETA for years, so I've seen the films and photographs of what animals go through for the most frivolous reasons, which, of course, includes fashion. Being raised that way, knowing that cruelty to animals was something to actively avoid, had an impact on my career. Before accepting a job with Chloe, I was offered so many different labels to work with, but what I've seen done to cattle killed for their hides and to raccoons and mink and other animals, made me say no if not using fur and leather was an issue. In the beginning, I might have thought, "Oh, god, I would really like to work in that house. I wish I wasn't so stubborn," but I knew I could never be happy selling out my integrity. I think I've said "no" more than I've said "yes" when faced with a chance to advance myself at the expense of my beliefs. I'm actually quite proud that I stuck to my decision never to touch the products of such outright cruelty. In fact, I sent the PETA video to every designer with an appeal to please stop using fur, at least. Karl Lagerfeld, rather predictably, felt he needed to return the video to me! Dolce & Gabbana were disgracefully rude about it, too. I frankly don't think most designers have the balls to watch animals writhing and being slaughtered; they don't want to admit they're responsible for such suffering.

What I find so bizarre is that some designers think they are so punk and rock when they use fur and leather, but there's nothing modern about it. In fact, most of the time, they are working furiously to make it all seem like something else. They take a beautiful fox and shave it and paint it pink and make it look like cotton corduroy. Or they take the skin that looked so amazing on the back of an animal and dye it green and make it look like plastic or some sort of print. How much saner to work with interesting technological creations if you want a modern look? You can mix linen and metal, for instance. There are a million fabulous fabrics: I can work with organic fibers in my collection; fabrics that can breathe, ones that let the heat out or hold it in; fabrics that move when your body moves, handwoven fibers. It's very exciting.

My designs are inspired by beautiful fabric, the amazing colors in a flower, a piece of music sometimes, a piece of embroidery. And me? I have been inspired by the goodness of my parents, I'm inspired by my husband and children, and I'm constantly inspired by the people I work with now. They're young and excited and cool and I admire them a lot. My rule in fashion is to have no rule in fashion. My rules in life are to be confident, be true to yourself, work hard, don't take yourself too seriously, and, most importantly, as my mother used to tell me when I was bullied at school or someone said I wasn't that great, "Don't let the turkeys get you down."

Making Purposeful Laughter

What would make a man roll a nut with his nose to the British prime minister's residence, walk around town in only his shorts and a snorkel, or wheel himself to Scotland in a shopping cart? In the case of Mark McGowan, it would be self-discovery and a desire to bring art to the masses.

I've always been drawn to people who engage others, who never forget that, no matter how far from each other our jobs or circumstances draw us, a sense of community, of being part of a bigger conversation, is important. That interest led me to talk to Mark McGowan, to find out what made him tick. And his story doesn't disappoint. Mark grew up in a rundown housing project in Peckham, England. As a youngster, he says, he would walk by the Camberwell College of Arts and dream of being a student there. It was a dream he didn't think would ever come true. After all, he was slipping into homelessness and would eventually end up "living rough" on the streets in any hole he could find. The slide was long, but thanks to a strange twist, not only did Mark McGowan end up at Camberwell College of Arts, he also now teaches a fine arts course there. I chose him to be part of this book because his story relates not only how Mark was spurred to overcome powerful odds, but how he used a cheeky style, and a tongue stuck firmly in his cheek, to inspire others to think about social issues that had often been invisible to them.

M y ordeal was like that of Sisyphus, pushing a boulder up a steep slope. Growing up, I found I had an addictive personality. So much so that I eventually became addicted to heavy drugs, alcohol, and anything else that was on offer. I seemed to turn up at every insane party from London to Ibiza, and I didn't seem able to stop the downward slide. There was nothing to motivate me to pull myself up, so I didn't. I would wake up late at night sweating, having passed out somewhere, shivering in some hole in the wall in an alley. I would drag myself out and swallow whatever warm dregs I found in my beer bottle, then crawl to the nearest bus stop and look for cigarette butts. I'd extract whatever tobacco I could find and roll it into something to smoke then crawl back into my hole. That was my life. In the end, I just lost my mind.

That's how I wound up in a mental hospital. I stayed there for eight years. In the hospital, we were given art therapy. Art was a great help. It gradually woke me up to what I wanted to do, to be. It gave me that most important rope to pull me out of the well: a sense of purpose. Nothing beats that. Taking one small step at a time, I tried to express myself through painting. I had to overcome the fears I had about myself, who I was, et cetera. Performance art seemed a good way to do that, to confront my own feelings. I discovered I was harboring a lot of shame, and that shame can give you anger. I didn't want to go around feeling angry, but with art, I learned, you can express that anger, go with it, and overcome it. Art works at all sorts of different levels. I now know I can't go out on the street thinking I'm going to change people with my ideas about discrimination, snobbism, waste, injustice, and so on. I have to open them up by opening myself up to them. My very first public performance consisted of taking my shirt off and walking across the street to buy a postage stamp. I was wearing swim shorts and a snorkel, so everyone stared. My body shape wasn't the best. I had a bit of a belly. But it was a breakthrough. I saw that people were embarrassed for me and that I was able to transfer what I was feeling about my appearance to them.

I've done all sorts of pieces since then, and been covered on the BBC and CNN and all over the world. There is a point to every piece. Part of it is how you set things up, getting the observers to think, to figure out what that point is. Engaging people, taking them out of themselves. It's an insane world with heavy issues pressing on us, so I try to find different ways to pose issues to people. I've stood for eight hours in the corner of an art gallery with a dunce's hat on and I've lain down in a doorway so that people had to use me as a doormat. You always get a reaction. Art is often insular, controlled, exclusive, but I can bring it to a far bigger audience, go out into the street and engage more than just those people who would feel comfortable or interested in going into a gallery.

I might roll myself along, or turn somersaults or cartwheels. Once I got down on my hands and knees on London Bridge and started crawling along, wearing a sign that said "Could you love me?" I went about sixty miles that way. Some kids threw stones, some people called me an idiot and demanded that I stand up, and some people offered me cups of tea. What I do really brings out people's characters, and that's part of it.

I like to laugh and so I try to bring a lot of humor to my art. I'll put chips on my head, tie bricks to my legs, or roll a bean or a nut along the pavement with my nose (I pushed a monkey nut to the front door of Number Ten Downing Street, the prime minister's residence, which made the press report that "There's now at least one nut at Number Ten"). There is always a serious element to my art, like making people think about why janitors are so poorly paid when they do such important work, or why we shouldn't waste water, but humor is a great leveler. I mean, imagine Osama bin Laden in a pink tutu! Being "silly" allows me to deliver something important to ordinary people in a way that makes them stop and talk about it all.

People become inhibited as they grow up; they lose their sense of wonder and that spontaneity they had as children. A child riding on the top of a double-decker bus will be looking at the sky, the bridge, his eyes bright, his mind going a mile a minute. I want to help restore those feelings, and I do. Instead of being stiff, people look over at me and laugh. Then they talk about what I'm doing.

Today I teach a fine arts course at Camberwell, the school I dreamt of attending when I was young. My class is composed of a special group of students aged from eighteen to seventy. I draw on my experiences now to enjoy each day, and I meet unique people every day that I'm performing, whole families, individuals. And all of them influence me. I don't want to ever be jaded. I keep in mind the story of a theatrical agent who has been in the business twenty-five years. An entertainer goes to his office and the agent says "What do you do?" so the entertainer runs across the room, swan dives out of the window, does the loop de loop in the air, comes back in, does a rolling handstand and then the splits. The agent looks up at him and says, "So, what else can you do?"

My answer is: I make art accessible to everyone.

You May Say I'm a Dreamer

Keith McHenry is an artist, activist, author, and public speaker. He is a cofounder of Food Not Bombs, which shares free vegetarian food in communities all over the world. He is currently listed by the U.S. State Department as one of America's 100 most dangerous people, and Food Not Bombs is listed on the FBI's Terrorist Watch List.

It is true that Keith has been arrested over 100 times. But it has been for "making a political statement" by sharing free food in San Francisco. He has spent over 500 nights in jail for his peaceful protests against militarism. He has also campaigned tirelessly to end police violence, cofounding October 22 as No Police Brutality Day.

Keith has been the keynote speaker at countless colleges including Oberlin and MIT and has spoken on topics such as fair trade and poverty in cities all across America, Mexico, Africa, Europe, Canada, and the Middle East. If this is a terrorist and a dangerous person, something is deeply wrong with our government's ability to tell a suicide bomber from a dumpster diver. I wanted Keith to tell his own story of how he became the man he is today.

My father worked for the Park Service, and I grew up in some of our most beautiful national parks. When I was in fourth grade, our family moved to Shenandoah, Virginia. Life became hard there, as I didn't fit in and the local kids would beat me up. It became frightening to go to school. I started to draw and paint around this time, and my father gave me a copy of *Walden* and *On Civil Disobedience* by Henry David Thoreau. The cruelty of my classmates changed me. I believe this is why I became a defender of the poor and oppressed. Reading *On Civil Disobedience* and learning about the war in Vietnam inspired me to choose nonviolent direct action for peace and social justice. While living in Shenandoah, we had mandatory Christian education at the public schools, and my parents went to the Parent Teacher Association meeting to ask that this violation of separation of church and state stop. The child of our town's only Jewish family had to sit by himself in the hallway during the Christian classes because the teachers were saying the Jews killed Jesus and it was upsetting to the young boy. The night my parents spoke out against forcing Christian education in public school a group of angry parents marched outside our house holding flaming torches, throwing rocks and yelling curses at my parents. My mother had us all go to a back room and pray for our safety. Not long after this horrific event Martin Luther King Jr. was killed in Memphis, Tennessee.

Later in life, while I was studying painting at Boston University, I heard Helen Caldecott speaking in Boston Common. She was standing on a milk crate telling a small group of people about the threat of nuclear war. Her talk inspired me to start doing public art addressing this issue. During the next few years, I met other antinuclear activists, and we thought we should use performance art to reach the public about the dangers of nuclear weapons and nuclear power. I designed a stencil of a nuclear mushroom cloud and the word "Today?" and my friends and I would spraypaint the image all over the Boston area. We also spraypainted the white outlines of dead bodies and messages of peace. Eight of us would organize public street events using puppets, music, movies, literature, and food as a kind of Living Protest Theater. The first time we dressed as military generals and tried to sell baked goods to buy a B-1 bomber. We found a poster that said, "Wouldn't it be a beautiful day if the Pentagon had to hold a bake sale to buy a B-1 bomber?" We also organized a soup kitchen outside the stockholders' meeting of the First Bank of Boston to protest their investment in the nuclear industry. We called this Food Not Bombs.

By 1980, it seemed like most peace and social justice groups were limited to speaking to one another and that each group had a narrow focus. In fact, we not only didn't talk with the public, our message was often boring and uninteresting. If we were going to change society, we needed to build a popular movement that mainstream America would be excited to join. To us the issues were all linked—be it El Salvador, homelessness, or nuclear power—and we felt if we helped make the connections between the way we live and the larger social issues, we might be able to build a larger movement. So, the founders of Food Not Bombs set out to make working for peace and social justice fun and easy for the public to join. We came up with a simple descriptive name that explained our principles. We designed a colorful, easy-to-recognize logo and we had a clear message and task that everyone could relate to. We collected food and fed the hungry, illustrating our belief that it's possible to solve social problems like hunger. Our office was a food and literature table on the streets at a busy intersection like Harvard Square. Thousands of regular people walked past us every day. We gave away free food, which was unique and enjoyable. People tended to visit our table longer when they stopped to get a bite to eat, and the food provided a way to teach people about the reasons we should eat organic vegetarian meals and work for peace, social justice, and animal rights. It was clear that our concept was working. People who had never heard of the peace movement before now knew they could stop by our table and learn about the organizations who never left their offices and about ideas and events that they would otherwise not know about. We built strong relationships with the people who lived in public housing or slept at the local battered women's shelters. Local city governments directed people to our project, and the mayor of Cambridge could be heard directing people our way when they needed assistance. Local grocery stores and bakeries also supported our work, and soon we were well connected with a community of people who had never had any relationship with the peace movement. Each day we picked up donated food from bakeries and grocery stores and delivered it to people at public housing developments, daycare centers, and battered women's shelters, and in the afternoons we would staff a table with food, literature, and T-shirts.

Over the years, we faced a lot of hard times, but perhaps the most difficult challenge was the ten-year struggle to share food in San Francisco. On August 15, 1988, nine of us were arrested for sharing food without a permit. We'd written the city requesting a permit, but after a number of failed attempts to get an answer, we started sharing food at the entrance to Golden Gate Park. Over forty riot police came out of the woods and surrounded our table, arresting those of us they saw giving away the food. The San Francisco Police made nearly 100 arrests that month but stopped when Mayor Art Agnos issued us a permit. The next summer the police started arresting the homeless in an effort to drive them from the city. Believing we were providing encouragement to the homeless, the mayor had the Health Department suspend our permit and the Recreation and Parks Department deleted the permit to share food in city parks. The mayor's office also took us to court, and we were ordered to stop sharing food and literature until we had a permit. We were arrested another 100 times until October 5, 1989, at 5:00 P.M., when the Loma Prieta earthquake rocked the Bay Area. That evening, instead of the police arresting us, they joined us for dinner.

All was well until after the election when the former chief of police, Frank Jordan, became mayor. He had run an anti-homeless campaign, and after he entered office, he started Operation Matrix and started arresting the homeless again. Food Not Bombs worked with the American Civil Liberties Union to document the abuse of the homeless, and we video-taped the police sweeps, capturing the confiscation of blankets, shoes, and other personal belongings, and the arrest of people for living outside. After one of our videos was aired on an Oakland TV station, the mayor ordered our arrest. This time we were charged with felony conspiracy to violate a court order to stop feeding the hungry. During the next three years, we were arrested over 700 times. The police often beat us, and on several occasions they tortured our volunteers. We organized a program where community groups, unions, and churches were invited to risk arrest one day a month. This helped us extend our campaign. In 1994, I was arrested under the new California Three Strikes law and faced twenty-five years to life. In all, I spent over 500 nights in jail. I was beaten thirteen times and tortured three times where my ligaments and tendons were ripped and I was placed in a small four-by-four-foot wire cage for three or four days. After the police smashed a club into my face, I had to have two surgeries to rebuild my tear ducts and sinuses. During this time, we would be arrested even when we weren't sharing food, adding to the stress. Our vehicles were towed and our equipment destroyed. The police also organized smear campaigns trying to discredit us, claiming we were rich and that our food was dirty and spoiled. The police infiltrated our group and tried to pit one member against another. One volunteer was so upset by the pressure he killed himself. The San Francisco Police wiretapped our home phones and followed our every move. Amnesty International declared our convicted volunteers "prisoners of conscience" and the United Nations Human Rights commission started an investigation into the human rights abuse against our volunteers. Finally, the city agreed to stop the prosecutions and the arrests. This had to be one of the most stressful times ever for my family and me. Even though the city spent millions of dollars trying to stop us, we not only continue to feed people in San Francisco to this day but people all over the world were inspired to start their own Food Not Bombs group in their community. So, while it was difficult, it was worth it. After the city stopped the arrests, many people expressed their gratitude. For some people the fact that we never gave up gave them great hope.

The most effective way to encourage people to support the ideas of Food Not Bombs is to set up a table and start sharing meals. The impact on people is powerful. When I was staffing a literature table in Tucson, Arizona, a woman with several children came up and told us that when she was homeless in Sacramento, California, she ate with Food Not Bombs. She regained her self-respect because of the way the volunteers at Food Not Bombs had treated her and her children. She said if it wasn't for Food Not Bombs, she might not have ever gotten off the streets, and she gave us $20.

There have been a number of times when someone visited our table and argued that a war is just or that homeless people should just get a job, and we spoke respectfully with them, sharing our ideas along with our food, and several years later they returned to say that something had happened to them and now they understand what we were talking about. A number of soldiers have been very angry with us, but when they return from war they tell us that they support our work and that war is wrong.

In 1989 I was arrested outside a developer's party at the University of California–San Francisco for "singing Christmas carols without a permit." The officer talked with me as he drove me to jail to spend the night locked up, and he asked me several questions about why we were singing outside this party. That summer the officer came to our table in Civic Center Plaza looking for me. He told me that our trip to jail made a big impression and he retired from the force that morning. He gave us a $20 bill, thanked us for our work, and waved goodbye.

Musically Speaking

John McLaughlin is, unquestionably, one of the greatest musicians alive and a pioneer of what has come to be called "world music." His compositions are mind-bogglingly expansive and nonconformist, going beyond the boundaries of jazz, rock, and other established genres. To me, he has always seemed to express something deeper than music itself. Students and admirers of his work, who number in the many millions worldwide, often report feeling the same way.

John grew up in Yorkshire, England, and began playing the guitar when just a lad. In the sixties, he moved to the United States and worked with Miles Davis's electric group, among others. During this time he began exploring Indian culture, music, and religion and went on to found his own acoustic group, Shakti, which included many notable Indian musicians. John is a gentle, charitable, and kind person with a particular love of animals and concern for war-affected children. He is a fascinating man, but so reserved that I am very happy to have him open up to readers about what he believes music contributes to life. In my book, literally and figuratively, if anyone should know, it's John McLaughlin.

Music is a language. A language without words, but nevertheless a language. Music speaks about the human condition, about the relationships we have with the beings in this world and the Universe itself. Most of these subjects are actually unspeakable in words, though the poetic form is the closest form of speech to music, but can be obliquely or sometimes directly indicated in music. I believe that music is a language of the spirit, and as such has definitely encouraged me to pursue my research into the fundamental questions of existence.

I am often asked where my motivation or my desire comes from. This is essentially unanswerable. It's like asking "where does awareness come from?" My particular musical conceptions, however, can be traced to two aspects: my cultural upbringing, and my innate tendencies, neither of which are conscious choices we make at birth, unless you believe in karmic choice. Regarding my innate tendencies I can say nothing. Regarding my cultural background, I'm very fortunate in having elder brothers who influenced me from childhood. Philosophically and musically, I owe a large debt to them both. They encouraged me to question everything, including the ultimate questions about life itself. My mother, an amateur violinist, also encouraged me to broaden my outlook in many ways, not only in music. These were, and still are, determining influences in my life. For example, I recall one winter evening when my mother showed me the planet Mars from our window, and then she gave me a copy of *The Martian Chronicles* by Ray Bradbury. I was about twelve or thirteen years old at the time. This was just one small event out of many that shaped my particular character.

Part of that character is my endless hope for humanity. How can you not have hope for us? It is our natural state. We are all already on this path, this journey, and always have been, the same place we set out for when we came down from the trees. The spiritual masters say we already are headed for enlightenment, and always were; we just haven't realized it yet. Yet, even though we have hope, it needs translating into action. We all have responsibility for each other. I believe we are all confronted by similar problems. There are millions of people, however, who don't have the luxury of considering anything other than how they will survive this day. And, of course, many don't. We in the West, on the other hand, are blessed with many more opportunities that give us the possibility of considering personal transformation. Since we all have weaknesses that need transforming, we have a greater chance of accomplishing this. I don't need to list our weaknesses since we all know what they are if we are honest with ourselves: Egotism, hatred, indolence, selfishness, greed, the list is endless.

Not everything can be overcome with music, not all our foibles will disappear if we learn to play the guitar or the tabla, but I will say that learning a musical instrument is very healthy, even for amateurs. You get a quick and humbling experience when learning to play an instrument, and in diving deeply into music, you learn also that you know next to nothing. That's a very important experience, in my opinion! And there are so many lovely pieces of music in our world, from Mozart to Miles Davis; this list is not endless, but long. The wonderful thing about music is that people love music, whatever the style. Music speaks to us directly and reminds us where we all belong, and that we all belong together.

The Soul with the Soles

Arthur Mintz is a retired photographer who lives with his wife, Marjorie, in Saratoga. I read about Arthur's adventure in a newspaper one morning and was so captivated I called him immediately! As it turns out, I got him out of bed (he was on the other coast: Saratoga, California, not Saratoga, New York); the sun hadn't yet risen on his day. When he'd had his breakfast, I called again to ask him about the odd cargo he had hauled in gunnysacks to South America. His story is so simple and lovely that I wanted it to be retold in this book. It shows that if you look about you, there is always something you can do to reduce discomfort in the world.

It all started with this fellow, a missionary for Medical Ambassadors, who lives down the street from our house and is a friend of ours. He used to go back and forth to Venezuela, taking doctors and supplies to the villages there. My wife and I love to travel, so it crossed my mind that it might be enjoyable to tag along with him, take photos of the wildlife, that sort of thing. We flew to Caracas with him, then took a small plane into the interior. From there, we traveled by dugout canoe for about twelve hours to the little village of Los Garcitas. The journey along the water was wonderful. There were birds everywhere. At one point, we witnessed flocks of white herons on the embankment, looking for fish because the river had overflowed, taking the fish with it. There must have been over 1,000 of them! I took lots of pictures.

We arrived in Los Garcitas to find a small village of houses with tin roofs and mud floors. The people are poor, mostly banana farmers, and the women use an old foot-pedal Singer sewing machine to make clothes. Almost no one wears shoes, but I didn't think much of it until, sitting at lunch, one of the doctors pointed out a child who was wearing shoes. He said, "See that child? Shoes are very important. Most of the diseases the children get come from bacteria and parasites entering their bodies through the soles of their bare feet." I thought about that. It was most unusual to see a village child with shoes. Back home in California, not only did the children all have shoes but they didn't wear out the shoes, they grew out of them. And the shoes they discarded still had a lot of use in them. When I returned to the States, I put the word out, using some of my photographs of the barefoot village children. There was instantly a great outpouring of shoes of all kinds and sizes. I went across the street to the coffee company and got seven gunny sacks that the coffee beans came in, and filled them with shoes!

When we returned to Venezuela, we hit a snag. The Customs agents wouldn't let us take the shoes in to their country. I didn't speak the language and couldn't get anywhere with them. I suspected some sort of scam on their part, but there was nothing I could do to make them listen. Luckily, my friend and neighbor speaks fluent Spanish. He can also talk like a Dutch uncle, so he rattled off arguments to the inspectors at full blast, giving them no chance to answer back. Within fifteen minutes the shoes were cleared and we were waved past with a cheery, "Welcome to Venezuela."

When we reached the village, we couldn't just leave the shoes in a pile or there would have been a mad scramble.

Instead, we had the children come to us, one at a time, so we could fit them properly with a pair of shoes and sent them on their way. Their faces lit up like Christmas trees! A few children got sports shoes that lighted when their feet hit the ground. They couldn't believe it. One child's foot was badly diseased, so rotted away, that the bone was showing through the flesh. He chose his shoes and then we carried him to the doctor's office and sat him in a chair. The dead flesh was cut away from his foot, antibiotics were applied, and his foot was bound up. All that time, no matter what was being done to his foot, he wasn't about to let go of those shoes.

I know that some parents took the shoes and sold them to buy food, but no matter, even that meant some difference had been made in their lives. If you ask me what comes to mind about this little act of caring, I will offer you Jesus Christ's words: "Do unto others . . . ."

We Are All Made of Stars

The title of this essay comes from a Moby hit that he wrote in memory of the air attacks on the World Trade Center on his birthday, September 11. While it has other meanings, this title seems to sum up the potential for all of us to become something special. Moby, whose real name is Richard Melville Hall—his nickname comes from the tale of the white whale, written by his great-great-great uncle—lives his life by doing what moves him. He doesn't follow trends, but creates music that often goes against them. Because of this, his early years weren't easy ones, but he never gave up on himself or gave into pressure, and through this tenacity he helped revolutionize dance music. Since then, he has changed up his music as his own interests and tastes evolved, again, unconcerned with the commercial viability of following his vision.

Moby is understated: a diminutive, humble (he calls himself "a simpleton"), bald, and somewhat quizzical-looking man with big glasses. He dresses down, lives in a modest apartment, and leads a quiet life. He shows that going against the grain can often be the key to making a difference.

I grew up very poor in a very wealthy town (Darien, Connecticut), so my biggest goal back then was to do my best to make sure people did not notice how poor I was. A whole laundry list of people and things influenced me, all the way from when I was a child. For a start, although this isn't the whole list, there's punk rock, Christ, Pete Seeger, John Robbins (John Robbins refused his inheritance of the Baskin Robbins ice cream fortune because he thinks dairy is poison and dairy farming is cruel to animals), good public school teachers, and my mom. My mother was a Pantheist, in that she liked just about everything. As for my religion, when I was sixteen years old I embraced Taoism because I had a crush on a young woman who was into Taoism, but I didn't really look seriously into religion until I was in my early twenties. I still don't think of myself as a religious person, although I love the teachings of Christ. I find most institutional religion bureaucratic and secular. Any religious belief or teaching that is not based on humility and compassion should be looked at very skeptically and warily.

Two words, labels really, that I try to avoid are "spiritual" and "creative." I don't know why, but these words make me uncomfortable. Maybe because they try to encapsulate things that are un-encapsulatable. And oftentimes people who describe themselves as "spiritual" and "creative" tend to be kind of smug. So, even though I'm smug once in a while, I avoid those words!

If I could offer any advice to someone about making their business life count for something, I'd give them the deathbed question. Very simply, what do you want to remember when you're on your deathbed? This is a question that should guide all of our actions and choices. Have your own standards. No one on their deathbed wants to say to themselves: "I worked for forty years at a job that I hated because it was expected of me and made my parents happy."

The world is a complicated place, and to pretend that it's not is to do yourself and the world a great disservice. We can only understand things on a subjective level, so we should never conflate our opinions for objective truth and fact. One of the only things that we can do to make the world a better place is to prevent suffering when we can. So, that's what we should do.

I think it's good advice to avoid compromise as well as settling based on fear and insecurity, especially as regards work and relationships. Don't take yourself too seriously, be nice to people, be loving and kind and forgiving, have as much fun as you can, do work that you love, help those (people and animals) who can't help themselves, eat well, buy Donna Summer's greatest hits.

AIMEE MULLINS

Running on Cheetah Legs

Aimee Mullins, a runway model, actress, and athlete, has turned down more interviews than she has accepted, so I am very pleased that she agreed to contribute to this book. Her story is a perfect example of self-reliance and what one person can achieve when she is determined, even when starting with a literal "disability" and when other people are telling her it just can't be done.

I was introduced to Aimee by a mutual friend, a filmmaker, who told each of us that we'd like the other. It was my treat to talk to her and find common ground in even little things. For instance, we both find it completely silly that people who think nothing of doing such "unnatural" things as flying, putting gel in their hair, or eating canned pineapple from a distant land, can find it somehow upsetting when someone chooses to add sexy high heels to her artificial legs! Aimee will tell us how she helped revolutionize the amazing world of prosthetic feet and legs.

Some things don't make sense to me, such as why people don't allow themselves a dream; why people just exist rather than choose to actively live life. It's a verb that requires action, "to live." We can actively impact the direction of our lives; things don't just keep "happening" to us. I just hate apathy! I'm amazed by it, really.

I was born without fibula bones in both my legs, and had to have my legs amputated below the knee. Some people call it a "congenital birth defect" but the term *defect* makes me cringe. It's like you're already starting out with a deficit, rather than a potential to be different, to do something different as opposed to what's expected. I didn't see how wearing prosthetics was quite so different from being born with flaming red hair in a crowd of black-haired babies, or being of a different religion from that of every other child in your area. It's just the way it is, and our differences are as important in making us "human" as are our similarities. As far back as I remember, I was being prepared for the worst, told things like, "you'll never be able to ride your bicycle," "you'll never be able to run," and "it will take you years to learn to walk." Luckily, I never believed anyone who made those kinds of sweeping negative pronouncements. I always thought they were completely wrong, and they were. Only you get to put those kinds of limitations on your life if you choose to, and why would we choose to limit rather than to dream—and dream big?

When I was a child, I wore wooden prosthetic legs, which were really uncomfortable. I had to put my stump into a thick wooly sock that went into a wooden socket that caused sores and blisters, but it was what I had, so I lived my life with it. As a kid, all I wanted to do was go outside and play, like almost all kids I knew. No sooner was I home from school than I was out riding my bike or playing ball or swimming. That's why, when I was eight, I was as excited as if it had been Christmas morning, when I got my first "high tech" legs, made for swimming. I was expecting these magical waterproof legs that I could swim in, legs that would resist the rot of the wooden ones. But they were horrible! If I went off the diving board headfirst, I would end up coming out of the water feet first. That's because they were actually so waterproof that they were buoyant. As I wore them and broke them in, they developed hairline cracks around the knees that let water seep in, making them almost too heavy to deal with at all. When I exited the pool, you could almost see the water level in the pool go down, there was so much water in my legs! My father ended up drilling holes in the ankles so that the water could run out.

The legs were a nightmare for another reason, too. They were made of a bright white plastic, like a filled milk jug, and the foot part was a tacky neon peach color. It was humiliating to wear them. I would go to the beach in New Jersey with my parents. Usually, by the time we got there, we would have to sit at least 100 yards back from the sea because of the hundreds of people on the beach in front of us. To get to the sea, it was like running the gauntlet. No one could ignore this blinding glow of my legs as I raced as fast as I could to the water's edge. Maybe that's where I first learned to sprint.

The experience was incredibly uncomfortable. People didn't want to stare at me, but they couldn't help it. People are afraid of what they don't understand, they're often too embarrassed to ask questions, and so they nervously giggle or point. Ultimately, these experiences made me strong, because I realized that everyone has felt that way in their lives, no matter what; everyone has felt as if they were standing out from everyone else in an uncomfortable way. That eventual realization helped me triumph over my awkwardness and find what I believed to be attractive within myself. If you aren't comfortable with yourself, you're hardly giving anyone else a reason to be comfortable with you either. The fact that I figured this out earlier than a lot of people might have been because of those awful legs. There's truth to the saying that, "unless a man finds peace within himself, it is useless to seek it elsewhere."

Growing up, I never knew another amputee. I didn't identify with being part of any "community" of people who didn't have their own feet or anything like that. I was just me. I'd never even heard of disabled sports. Then, when I was in college, a guy I knew suggested that I compete in the National Disabled Sports Championships in Boston. At first, I was so offended. Having always played against kids who had natural legs, and proud of competing on championship teams, I thought I didn't need the cheap thrill or "esteem-boost" of being able to beat someone in a wheelchair, someone who couldn't use their legs! But obviously, I was truly ignorant about the whole disabled sports scene. At that time, I was more into painting and acting, but I did love sports. I couldn't resist finding out about this whole world I had never been a part of. Then I got to thinking. I was in my summer job at the Pentagon (not fun) and I figured if I could get approval to take the Thursday and Friday off to go to the Games, I could have a long fun weekend in Boston, which I hadn't seen before. I'd never even been in a sprint race at that time, and had no formal training, which left me to my own devices. My big idea was to have no caffeine for a couple of weeks. Then, the morning of the race, I drank a big coffee to get me going, thinking I'd have some extra pep in my step. Of course, that was a ridiculous idea since I already felt like throwing up because I was so very nervous, not knowing what awaited me. I asked an official if he had any last minute advice and he said, "Honey, if at the end of the race you have anything left in you, you didn't run hard enough." So, when the starter's pistol went off, I threw myself down that track. I ran as if something big and hairy was chasing me, and I won, literally by a nose, my nose pushed over that finish line. I had beaten the national record holder by just six hundredths of a second!

After the race, I met Van Phillips, a prosthetics designer of carbon graphite legs with shock absorbers for cross training (what I affectionately call "Robocop legs"). He gave me his card and told me I needed to train properly—as a runner. I ended up calling him a few months later and asking him to give me some of those high-tech fancy legs. The insurance companies only give you very basic legs, but I wanted legs that would help me become what I wanted to be, the fastest woman on artificial legs in the world. As a kid, I had watched *The Bionic Woman* on TV and whenever they said, "We can rebuild her," my heart would flutter. I wanted to be sensual, feminine, and superfast, just like her. I was an athlete, and I wanted to be the best. What I didn't know was that I wasn't going to get that Robocop leg, I was going to get something much better for sprinting. The idea for the "cheetah leg" came about because, after all these years of trying to mimic human legs with prosthetics, we started looking at the fastest thing that runs.

Whereas most prosthetic legs can be modeled from a person's other leg, matching the weight, calibration, alignment, height, and so on, I am missing both legs, and it's hard to match against something that's not there. In my case, the "lack" of something resulted in an area of potential, where we could create whatever we wanted to try and fulfill our dreams of being fast. Van developed the Flex-Foot "cheetah leg," a simple C-shape design that weds technology to nature and, with the materials of woven carbon fiber, actually improves upon it, allowing a human amputee to push beyond what his or her body would have done naturally.

Nothing great is going to happen unless you start making it happen, and that almost invariably involves risking something, whether it's time, money, energy, or pride. Because of that collaboration with Van, I succeeded in becoming one of the fastest women on the planet, and sports prosthetics were revolutionized. Now I'm getting to working with scientists at MIT Media Lab on testing the first powered ankle, which is like the Holy Grail of leg prosthetics! It would be a huge gift to get some ankles that work.

It's a privilege to be considered a pioneer, but I'm no martyr. I didn't choose what I started out with, I just decided that

I wanted to be the very best I can be. In my little journal of sayings is my longtime favorite: Gandhi's words, "You must be the change you wish to see in the world." Stop complaining about what is missing in your life and start dreaming and doing and filling that void you noticed in the first place.

When I went on Oprah's show, she bent down and examined my artificial legs. She then looked up at the audience and said, "I will never complain about having to get on the treadmill at the gym again!" The audience laughed along with her. I didn't really see the point of why she thought that my having prosthetic legs equated to me loving to get on the treadmill. I said to her, "Why? I hate the treadmill as much as you all do and I go to the gym for the same reason you all do. Because my ass would weigh 300 pounds if I didn't!" (I love food!) And that's how it is. I'm going through the same things as everyone else, I get afraid the same as anyone else, and I want to look good like everyone else. If I'm known for my talent, I think that does more to change the idea of what it is to have a "disability" than if I am an object of misdirected sympathy. Feelings are universally human. I feel the sting of being too proud, or of being scared, or the responsibility that comes with succeeding—you have to keep dreaming bigger, and resist that urge to censor yourself and your wildest imagination. I am forging through this life just like everyone else. Perhaps the only difference for me is that I can be any height I want to be and put on the most gorgeous pair of high heels you can imagine, just by putting on a different pair of legs!

Champion of Fair Play

There is no doubt that one of the best things ever to happen to U.S. tennis was the 1975 defection from Czechoslovakia of Martina Navratilova, the young woman who would dazzle the sport. Described by Billie Jean King in 2006 as "the greatest singles, doubles and mixed doubles player who's ever lived," Martina Navratilova holds the all-time record for the most titles held—for men or women—having won eighteen Grand Slam singles titles and forty-one Grand Slam doubles titles, as well as the women's singles title at Wimbledon nine times.

Martina's athletic prowess alone is reason enough for inclusion in this book, for she has a determination and passion for her sport that is motivating and inspiring. Yet, there is something else to admire about her: Martina is forthright. Born in a communist country, seeking citizenship in her new home, working to be a credit to her gender and more, she has had to wait patiently for the moment when she could finally speak openly and honestly about her political beliefs and about her sexuality. A caring and driven individual, although now retired from professional tennis, Martina still inspires good sportsmanship and champions human and animal rights.

learned to play tennis when I was about five years old, hitting the ball up against the wall outside my home. I used my grandmother's racquet (she called me her "little golden girl") and it was so heavy that I had to grasp it with both hands.

168

That's how I developed my backhand, slamming the ball that way into the wall! It was about two years before I played on a real court. A coach recognized my talent and took me under his wing, training me for free. If he hadn't, we would never have been able to afford lessons. He told his wife, "She's going to be a champion," but he never told me. I only found that out much later. I had a huge crush on him. His name was George and he was tall, blond, handsome, sweet, and sexy. His nickname was "Gorgeous George." I also had crushes on girls, but if I could have been with him, I might have been straight!

Tennis is exhilarating, very exciting. Billie Jean probably said it best when she said something to the effect of, "I've been playing for years and I've never seen the ball come over the net the same way twice." You have to constantly adjust your playing to get it just right. In some other sports there's more of a set situation, few or no variables. In tennis there's always a need for a new reaction. When the ball's coming at you, you have to react and consider, in a split second, the surface, the opponent, the wind, all sorts of factors. I've never understood how Venus [Williams] could say she is bored after forty-five minutes. It's always different, always exciting.

I believe in fairness. That's what I was taught as a child, to play fair, to be fair in all things, and that's what I try to do. I can get livid if I think something is unfair and so I've had to learn to control my temper. It has even cost me matches. For example, if it were up to me, there would be no linesmen. If there was a doubt, I'd give the benefit of it to my opponent. I would expect my opponent to do the same for me. But some people don't return such courtesy! It used to be, in the old days, that if I got a bad call, I'd get extremely upset at the injustice of it. Or if I missed an easy shot, I'd mope, whine, and moan about it. I might miss one point for the mistake or the bad call, but I'd end up losing three or four games or the whole match because of my mood. Then, someone else in professional sports said to me, "You're only hurting yourself really. The newspapers won't say 'Oh, Martina lost the match because of an unfair call that upset her.'" I realized she was right. No one but me knew what was throwing my game; it was stupid. So, after that, I effectively controlled my anger.

The more I think about it and talk about it, the more that I see that my reasons for leaving my country combined two important elements of who I am. Staying would have meant not having the freedom to play tennis as I wanted to, and it was such a taboo to be gay. I was living under a repressive regime with total control. If you wanted to leave the country, you had to get a visa from a foreign embassy, but before you crossed that bridge, you had to have permission from the national authorities to apply for one. No permit from them, no visa. The federal government could nominate me to go to a tournament or deny me permission. I had played doubles with Chris Evert, that sort of thing, and the authorities were concerned that I was becoming "too Americanized," too influenced by a free society. They were right: I was having a hard time living in my own country and I knew I had to get out one way or another. The authorities had OKed me to go to the European tournament, but it seemed clear that I wasn't going to be allowed to play in the U.S. Open again. Then, suddenly, my break came and the officials at the tennis federation let me go to New York only for a week before the tournament. I seized my visa and left. As soon as I lost to Chris in the semifinals, I defected.

I couldn't "come out of the closet" as early as I wanted to. First, I was applying for U.S. citizenship and being gay would have disqualified me. And being famous brings its own problems. Sometimes someone a celebrity has a relationship with doesn't want to be in the spotlight, perhaps because they are not ready to "come out" themselves or simply because, gay or straight, they want to be private people, not public property. That's how it was with me with my partner. I remember, too, when Chris and I were up for the presidency of the World Tennis Association, back in 1979 or 1980, and we had to give a special spiel to the committee. I said, "By the way, I'm in a relationship with a woman." They wanted to know if I was going to tell the press. I said that if asked, I would answer truthfully. Needless to say, I didn't get the presidency! That wasn't long after the Billie Jean "scandal," so there was always the threat that the sponsors would pull out of the women's tour and that would be the end of it.

In the end, I did answer a newspaper reporter's question. I told him that I was bisexual (the way we put it back then) but asked him please not to write anything at that time until after the Monte Carlo exhibition, as I didn't want to hurt the tour. The next day, despite his assurance that he would not write the story, it was out. The reporter said that his editor had pressured him. Back then, it was a huge scandal, and it was touch and go for the tour's main sponsor. Now, when people ask me, I advise them to always try at least to come out to their friends and family. Your friends are your chosen family, so they should support you, even if others don't. And, although each situation is different, by coming out you can help others around you feel more comfortable and supported if they're struggling in that way. As for youngsters, I advise to always have an escape hatch if you decide to come out to your parents, because they might throw you out of the house for being gay. You had better have a relative's or good friend's place where you can stay, just in case.

I have never felt ashamed of being gay, even when people have tried hard to make me feel that way. I know how I feel isn't wrong. There can be nothing wrong with loving another human being, regardless of their gender. What is wrong is to be prejudiced against those you don't understand or who don't feel exactly like you. Occasionally, someone will throw the Bible at me and I say, "Are you saying that God had us evolve in every way over the last two thousand years but the Bible has not?" I ask them to look at the Bible. It justified human slavery, genocide, the sacrifice of animals. We've evolved beyond those things! The Bible has evolved in those things, why not in human sexuality? Then they might say, "Well, it's not normal." I think of Naomi Judd's words. She said, "Normal? Normal is just a cycle in a washing machine." You can have a normal temperature, a normal water level, but what is a normal human being when we are so full of emotion, love, and sexuality?

Being visible has helped give gay people strength, but I think what matters is not whether I'm gay or straight, but that I stand up for who I am and what I believe. I'm not outspoken, but I say what I think and often say what others think, too, but are afraid to say. Apparently this makes me "outspoken" and even controversial! So, while what I say may be completely "normal" or at least acceptable ten or twenty years from now, it does not help me now when it comes to being marketable. I was recycling batteries decades ago and I bought stock in Whole Foods ten years ago.

My fans seem to come from all corners of the world as well as all corners of society. Anyone oppressed likes me for sticking up for the underdog, but there are many other pockets of fandom: Straight housewives go crazy. They say, "Oh, Martina, we love you!" and I think "Whoa there!" Kids tell me they love the way I play and they think it's super cool that I'm older than their moms and I'm beating a woman half my age. There's an old conservative man from Utah who has watched me play for years and has become my pen pal! Diversity is the great and wonderful thing about life.

I try to be a good role model by being a consummate athlete setting an example in that way. I advocate eating nutritious food (I'm a vegetarian), working out, being in top form mentally and physically, and by cultivating a team of positive people around me. One of my strengths is in listening to advice from people I trust. For example, if my coach told me to change my stroke, I would put that change to work that very day, not in a week or a month. I'd make it start working for me then and there. I also have a knack for selecting what bit of advice, perhaps one piece out of ten, is relevant for me in the moment. Years later, a light bulb might go off and I will think "Ah, that other advice can work for me now," because everything has its time. W. Somerset Maugham once said, "Only average people are at their best every day." I love that! Never hang back and play it safe because you fear that you'll fail. To me, the only failure is the failure to try. Most people can do more than they think they can, so go ahead, push that envelope. It's like they say, "nothing ventured, nothing gained."

Greasing the Wheels to American Self-Reliance

"Hi, it's Willie," he says when he calls, and from among the billions of people on the planet, you know there is only the one. His voice is unmistakable, and like Willie himself, it seems to smile down the line at you. I have loved the man since I first heard him sing "Good Times" in 1968. You can just tell he's fun, he's irreverent, and, well, he's just plain decent. His big heart includes a mile-wide soft spot for the state of Texas and for people everywhere who are like those he grew up around—hardworking and hard playing and looking out for each other.

Willie could have left those good ole country values behind when he hit the big time or later when he settled in Hawaii, but he never did. He campaigns for the little guy—and for the horses, too, helping close down U.S. slaughterhouses that cater to the horsemeat market overseas. His story is about the power of one person to keep on remembering what's important in life, no matter how high up the ladder you climb, a value a whole lot of "rich folk" sadly forget. That's why I am happy to include Willie in this book.

I was born in Abbot, Texas, just twenty miles away from where my old friend Carl Cornelius runs a truck stop. Abbot, like most Texas towns, is a small and special place. It's a farming community, and when I was a boy it consisted of about 300 people, and I think it still does! We all knew each other; we kids went to school together, we worked the fields together, and played ball together, all that kind of thing. I grew up thinking everyone in the world was like me, because everyone around me sure was. It wasn't unusual to care about everything going on with everyone, and because of that I'm particularly not inclined to sit back and watch what's going on around me. I participate. As a born troublemaker, you might say that I have been dumb enough, nervy enough, and nosey enough to be into everything!

Carl and I go way back. Some forty or so years ago, I met him through another of my friends, Zeke Varnon. Zeke has been a huge bad influence on me; we used to run around, gambling, drinking, and having a high old time. Then I kind of lost touch with him until, one day, I was driving along the highway from Dallas to Waco and what did I see but a billboard with a picture on it of Zeke, Carl, and . . . me! It was advertising Carl's Corner Truck Stop. I knew Zeke and I knew Zeke's tricks, but I didn't know Carl until that day. I stopped and went in the place and met Carl and we had a lot of fun. I found out that he had started the truck stop just so that there'd be somewhere a person could get a drink in this dry county, a hangout where truckers coming up and down the highway could get something to eat, play some cards, and have a good time. Ever since then, I've been fond of that place, and I've watched it go up and down, from good times to bad and back again.

Let me explain how this is tied to my bio-fuels idea. It was actually my wife, Annie, who started this. She asked me what I thought about her buying a Volkswagen Jetta that ran on bio-diesel. I asked "What's that?" I was a bit leery at first, but as soon as I heard that this stuff came from 100 percent vegetable oil my mind started to race. I instantly thought of the family farmers who are going under, who can't make ends meet, the very reason I started Farm Aid back in 1985. There are fields full of cotton in Texas, and here was enormous potential for a new use for the cottonseed, as well as a reason to grow more soy or corn, because all that can become bio-fuel. Here was a way to boost the farmers' income, to shine a light at the end of the tunnel for those farmers. For them, times get harder and harder, but with bio-fuel they could make money again.

I got together with these two great people, Bob and Kelly King, man and wife from Maui, real pioneers in bio-fuels who had started Pacific Bio-diesel, and I learned a whole lot. They actually go around and collect used vegetable grease from restaurants all over Hawaii, where I have a house, and they recycle it into fuel. I learned how good bio-fuel is for the environment, how it costs less, gives better mileage, your engine runs smooth, it can go in anything that has a diesel engine, and it's biodegradable. The other thing that resonates with me is that if Americans can produce it from homegrown crops, we can stop depending on foreign oil. Everyone knows that we went to war with Iraq for the oil; it has the second largest oil holdings in the world, but there's no excuse for killing people over oil. There's no need to start wars over oil when we can grow our own. I put a 300-gallon tank up at my house and we run the vehicles on bio-fuel, including my Mercedes. Every household can put a tank by the garage. When you run your car, the exhaust will smell like peanuts or cracked corn! The potential is huge, and the surface hasn't even been scratched yet.

Carl was going through a bad personal patch right about the time I was learning all about bio-fuels, and he was thinking of closing the truck stop down. I got hold of him and said we could do something. How would he like Carl's Corner to be the first place in the United States to sell "Bio-Willie" at the pumps? We started with just a bit of it, hoping it would sell, but it took off like a rocket. I was on XM Satellite radio with another old friend, Bill Mack, who hosts the *Open Road* show, and we started talking to truckers about bio-diesel. Word spread up and down the highway and soon everyone was pulling into Carl's to try it. Now we are building a bio-diesel plant right next to the truck stop. It'll be run by all local-based people from the community, so people who were thinking of quitting the area can stay and make some money.

Change is all about thinking positively. What you think is what you'll be, so I try to be positive, and that's what I tell all the kids. By concentrating on the possibilities, you attract good things. Bio-fuel is one of those good things.

Put a Little Love in Your Heart

Petra Nemcova always wanted to be a model, and after being spotted in a national talent contest, her dream came true. Her beautiful countenance (and body) has since appeared on the covers of, among others, Bazaar, Sports Illustrated, *and* Cosmopolitan; *she has starred in videos for* Vogue; *writes editorials for* Elle; *hosts the TV show* A Model Life; *and was hand-chosen by designers including Valentino and Armani to work the catwalk in their favorite creations. In 2005, her world was turned upside down. She was vacationing on the Thai coast with her fiancé, Simon Atlee, when the tsunami struck. Her beloved Simon was washed away and drowned, and although Petra survived, she was badly injured. It took great resolve for her not to succumb to her emotional and physical injuries, but she succeeded. Her professional comeback was celebrated as complete when, in 2006, she was featured again in the* Sports Illustrated *swimsuit issue. Her long-standing personal determination to help others, particularly children, was only strengthened by her experience. Love has become a Hallmark card word, bandied about casually and often without a grain of sincerity, but in Petra's case love is the word that guides her conduct. In 2005, she launched the Happy Heart Foundation to help youngsters who suffer loss or hardship in disasters all over the world.*

My childhood was a happy one. Although we weren't rich financially, it left me with many rich memories, memories that I rely on to get me through rough times. For instance,

I remember that my grandfather used to bake delicious cakes. There was one in particular that was fabulous: a flat cake full of fruit with a sugary crust. My sister and I couldn't resist eating it while it was still hot, and so my grandfather would make us whistle tunes because if we were whistling, we couldn't be eating! When I have especially down moments, when something in my life gets too oppressive or stress attacks me, there's one treasured scene I return to in my mind. It's of me when I was eight or nine years old, sitting on a hill in high grass, looking down into a beautiful valley. I used to pick mushrooms in that area by myself, and I'd roll down that hill for the sheer joy of it. The scene is so peaceful and comforting that it calms me.

I have always wanted to bring happiness to people, to help them, especially children. I'm so appreciative of what I have in my life. I knew what I wanted to do from the time I cut apart my mother's skirts and stitched them into clothes I'd want to wear, and my career has been a steady rise. Some girls become only runway girls, but I have succeeded in commercials, catalogues, and editorials, in all sorts of ways as well as on the runway. That gives me a good balance, and I'm grateful for being so lucky. I know that any of us can help others no matter what we have, but it's wonderful for me to have so much good fortune that I can share.

My ordeal in Thailand when the tsunami struck was a true test of my belief in the power of love and positivity. It was a terribly hard experience, for me certainly, but also for millions of people who were affected in so many countries. When the waves hit our beach at Khao Luk, the love of my life, my fiancé, Simon Atlee, and I were in our bungalow. The water came in and we were swept away in seconds. There was instantly debris everywhere: bits of broken building, wood, trees, objects. I was dragged down and under and debris was hitting me, causing internal injuries and breaking my pelvis. I tried kicking my

way out, but the water was black and I was going down, not
up. I thought, "This is it, I'm meant to go." I accepted my fate,
trusted that whatever would happen would happen and stopped
struggling. I can't explain it, but I felt suddenly peaceful. In fact,
it was the most peaceful moment of my life. When someone
says "go with the flow," I know now what they mean, exactly!

Almost at once, I saw blue sky, and I was on the surface
of the water again. I managed to reach a tree and cling there
for almost eight hours. Around me, I could hear children
screaming, adults crying out. After about thirty minutes, the
children couldn't hang on, they were not strong enough, and
the screaming died down as they drowned. The worst thing
was that I couldn't go and help them because my broken pelvis didn't allow me to move. The wonderful thing was that
all around me strangers were working hard to save everyone.
Even though they knew that another wave might come in, that
didn't stop them trying to rescue people they didn't know, had
never met. There were so many helpers, reaching out to others
at the risk of their own lives.

In those long hours in the tree, I worried about Simon,
whether I would ever see him again. He was so gentle and
kind and always laughing and helping others laugh. I clung
there, sending out energy, prayers, and good thoughts to all the
people in difficulty. I wasn't angry at Nature, but I knew this
was a very big event. Of course, I only found out later just how
big it was.

From what I have heard, it takes most people at least two
years to heal from the kind of injuries I had. But I took three
and a half months because of the energy work I did and my
strength of mind. The mind is a very powerful tool, and you
can easily enter a downward spiral of depression and negative
thoughts. I wanted to get stronger, not weaker, to heal emotionally and physically, so I did not allow it to look at the minuses,

only the plusses. It is always a choice, and I chose to concentrate on getting stronger, on appreciating all I have. I still had loved ones, I had my sister, my mother; I could breathe, I could feed myself, eventually I could walk. I was very lucky, and all I wanted to do was get well enough to go back and help others. You can die any time. Poof, you are gone. So, if you are alive, I think it's best to make the most of it. We all have to go through hardships, maybe not a tsunami but something else devastating to us, and there will always be something good that comes from it, whether 50 percent or 1 percent. You can concentrate on that good bit. In the tsunami, I remember all the unconditional love that flowed from it, all those who helped each other because of it, the amazing and spontaneous unity we saw in its aftermath. That is very powerful.

The heart is the key to everything good. I began Happy Hearts Foundation to help children who have suffered loss or hardship as a result of natural, economic, or health-related disasters in many different countries, not just Thailand. It not only makes them happier but makes me very happy, too. I think the world would be a very different place if we didn't think of me, me, me and thought of we, we, we. It would make us less likely to take and take and take and more likely to give and give and give. If I could be granted one wish, it would be to convert "me" into "we." That way, we could fill our hearts with love and kindness and there would be no room left for fear or hate.

WADE RATHKE

Powerful Communities from Little ACORNs Grow

Wade Rathke is chief organizer and founder of ACORN, the Association of Community Organizations for Reform Now, a grassroots group that has a long history of lifting up the working poor. Wade calls me "Sister Newkirk," a reminder that he has been a workers' organizer almost all his life! I admire Wade because he has devoted decades to working for the underdog, even when quaking in his boots and doubting his own ability to succeed. Wade's underdogs are people who need help in pulling themselves up out of poverty. He has made a crucial difference to millions by organizing whole neighborhoods to lobby, vote, and protest; he's helped them unite to secure a living wage, protect workers from environmental hazards, disrupt professional loan sharking, even to get a traffic light installed at a dangerous intersection.

Years ago, Wade helped create the "People's Platform," to lobby for fair treatment for the poor, capturing the support of the Reverend Jesse Jackson. Marching onto national park land, he established tent cities for the homeless that no politician could ignore, then marched on Washington with thousands of people whose basic needs were being ignored even as military and other spending increased overseas, Starting from scratch, but drawing around him a legion of "sisters and brothers," Wade has secured the rights of the often disenfranchised and forgotten underclass of, first, the United States, and now other countries too. I'm including him because his story can empower us all.

was born in Laramie, Wyoming, but my dad worked for the California Company (now Chevron) and was transferred frequently, so I spent my childhood more or less on the road from Colorado to Montana to New Mexico to Kansas. We finally settled in New Orleans, but that sense of rootlessness had a big influence in my life, as did the public high school I attended. My class was the first to be integrated outside of the elementary grades in New Orleans because under "separate but equal" there were no equivalent African-American high schools. Most high school teams would not play our high school in sports after integration. This and the time spent in Mississippi watching the impact of what was happening in the Delta where my grandmother and cousins lived and where race was a big issue, forced me to have to think about where I stood and what I thought about issues like human equality.

This was in the mid-1960s, and civil rights and the Vietnam War were all that anyone talked about. After high school, I worked one summer offshore of Louisiana. Late at night, I would get into vigorous debates with some of the guys who worked with me, and many of them, twice my age, would look at me at the end of the debates, nod their heads in agreement and say that they would never let their kids go to Vietnam. All of this got me thinking, and it seemed that I either needed to do something about all of this or just bust wide open!

I attended the Spring Mobilization in 1967 in New York and heard Martin Luther King and others speak, and I was one of the thousands who marched to the Pentagon in early 1968. I wanted to make a difference somehow, but I didn't know how. I dropped out of college, was trained briefly by the Boston Draft Resistance Group, and went back to New Orleans to see if I could organize working people like us to understand their rights in dealing with the war. It was a hard time for six months, because I didn't really know what I was doing and had to take a clerk and lift-truck-driver job at a coffee plant to make ends meet. After six months, I gave it up, got married, and headed for California, where we camped along the coast for a few months. I was filled with rage over injustice, but didn't have a place to plant it. Then, that summer, a woman tracked me down to ask if I would be an organizer for the National Welfare Rights Organization (NWRO). I grabbed the opportunity and never looked back.

I founded ACORN in June 1970 in Little Rock, Arkansas, as a special, experimental project of NWRO, but within six months ACORN and the NWRO parted ways over our different priorities, leaving us without even two cents to rub together, no office, no salaries, and for the most part a staff cobbled together from volunteers. I started the membership dues system with ACORN, simply telling everyone the truth: if our members didn't pay dues, the organization would go under. The notion of poor, working families paying dues was heresy in those days, but it was either that or close up shop. And it worked. People paid dues so that ACORN would survive, and that's been the basis of the organization ever since that time.

If anyone thinks all this just happens effortlessly, let me say there is never a day when I am not plagued with worries and doubts! In Springfield, when I was first beginning to build NWRO, I had migraines so bad that I was convinced I had a brain tumor and actually walked into a free clinic in the Riverview Gardens public housing project and asked the nurse what the symptoms for such a tumor might be. In Little Rock and a thousand other times when everything seemed to be on the line, I had a pit in my stomach as large as a grapefruit. I have found no cure for such fear when the weight of responsibility is on you and it matters to thousands whether the organization wins or loses, whether your quest and theirs succeeds or fails.

You simply have to gut it out and work right through it to the other side.

Is it worth it? Definitely. Recently, an outside researcher assessed ten years of ACORN's major victories from 1995 to 2004 as having delivered $15 billion worth of benefits to low- and moderate-income families and neighborhoods. In the November 2006 election we won minimum-wage increases that we had brought to the ballot in initiatives in Ohio, Arizona, Missouri, and Colorado, which delivered raises to 4.5 million low-wage workers worth over $6 billion. Whether winning better drainage, new parks, stopping loose dogs, compelling banks to invest in low-income neighborhoods, improving schools, or 1,000 other things, each of these accomplishments has meant the world to some of our members. This work has given my life purpose and meaning, and I am so happy to have had the opportunity and ability to start and stay with one organization for the last thirty-seven years! I now serve more than 250,000 family members.

The motto for ACORN is borrowed from the state motto of Arkansas: The People Shall Rule! That has always sounded just right to me. There's another motto on my desk that essentially says: work hard and organize. And at the end of my blog it says, "You take it from here to there." All of these things seem right to me. I have tremendous belief in and respect for the value and ability of the "uncommon common people" that make up the low- and moderate-income constituency and ACORN's membership.

ACORN's first president, Steve McDonald, used to constantly advise us as we were growing "not to get the big head," which was pretty sound advice. Social change is about sweat. It's constant perspiration rather than sudden inspiration that wins victories and builds organization. I believe the day we lose ground is the day we don't go to work, and that as long as we're fighting and struggling to win every day, we have a chance. My best advice to anyone who wants to be an organizer is to always be ready for hard work, expect no thanks and no quarter, and make sure that every day adds up to some kind of progress, so that in putting it all together we collectively have the opportunity to win.

DORIS RICHARDS

Fighting for a Dog Park

Doris Richards's name may not be a "household" term, but a lot of people—and a lot of dogs—owe her a debt of gratitude because the term dog park *is one. The concept of a dog park is relatively recent, and "Doris's dog park" was the first of its kind, though I'm happy to report there are now thousands upon thousands of them across the country. Its proper name is the Ohlone Dog Park, located in Berkeley, California, where Doris has always lived, sometimes with dogs, sometimes without. Doris's idea to create this special place was not an instant smash hit. Although Doris lives in such a dog-friendly community that in some churches dogs are not only welcomed but even take communion, there was opposition to her idea. From nervous neighbors to financial interests who didn't want dogs digging in the land they wanted to buy or sell, some folks were determined there would never be a dog park in Berkeley. But Doris is the sort of woman who doesn't go away, tail between her legs. In fact, she's a bit like a dog herself; like one who can almost taste that cookie you have all to yourself and therefore plants himself right there, looking pointedly from the cookie to you, you to the cookie, until you give in and share. Apart from the fact that I believe dogs need parks as much as bees need flowers, Doris's tenacity and willingness to make her dream into reality is why I chose her for this book.*

A couple of decades ago, there weren't any dog parks in San Francisco. In fact, there weren't any dog parks anywhere. If you were near the Golden Gate Park, where I live, and you shared your life with a dog, there were a couple of dog "runs," that's all. It was a matter of "go potty and go home."

One day, the city decided to tear out blocks of houses. They were going to build a rapid transit station or parking lot there or something. I don't think they had decided exactly what to do with that land. But, as soon as they filled it in with dirt, people started to flock there, and many of them brought their dogs. The area takes up about half a city block and is far enough off the road, so it was a great place to let the dogs loose and know they could run safely. And, of course, everyone started chatting, and all the people with dogs got to know each other. It was very friendly.

We were experiencing troubled times back then, with the police clamping down on free speech in Berkeley. A group called "People's Park Annex" would hang out in the empty area, having picnics and—whenever someone was arrested for protesting against the war—collecting bail money. The police didn't like this, so they put fences up around the park. But the "radicals" cut the fences in strategic spots. It was also discovered that if enough people leaned against the fence at once, it fell over and the park was opened up again. In went people with their dogs! All day long, there must have been twenty to twenty-five dogs coming and going from that place at a clip.

Of course, we all wanted to save that land from being developed and to keep it a place where the dogs would be able to be themselves once in a while. So there was a panic when, one day, we heard they were going to take it all away. There was some plan to build a community college, although no one in the area wanted all the traffic that would come with it. We decided to petition the city to turn that land into a dog park. No one had heard the term before. They kept saying "a run"? "No," we'd say, "a park. For dogs."

I had had back surgery and I wasn't working, so I offered to help get people organized. We formed a club, had meetings, and became a force to be reckoned with. Funnily enough, I wasn't able to join the club, as I didn't have a dog then and you had to have a dog to be part of it. But they let me go to meetings. At first, someone else was president, but then I got a husky named Killik and they made me president.

This was my first taste of civic activism. It took a lot of work. I didn't mean to get into it, but I felt useless sitting home after my back surgery. With this project, I could do things even though I had an odd schedule, and it made me feel useful. We found all sorts of allies, including at Animal Control and in the Parks Department. The head of the Parks Department started out worried but in the end, got to know the dogs and became a big advocate. By 1983, the City had heard all our arguments. They made the decision to see how the dog park idea worked, to make it an experiment.

Just before opening day, trees were delivered to make the park look pretty for the opening ceremonies with the mayor and everyone. But because it was fall, when the trees arrived they lost their leaves overnight. So, we spent hours stringing leaves on them, orange and red leaves like those on an artificial Christmas tree! On the big day, it took the head of the Parks Department a while to realize the leaves were all false.

It turned out that we weren't home free, however. In fact, it's been a constant struggle to keep our dog park. You have to be vigilant. New people move in, knowing there's a dog park, and then complain to the City that dogs bark and the park makes them nervous and other stupid things. I mean, if you move in next to an airport, expect airplanes. One day, the City posted an innocuous little notice, just one little notice in the park. Someone took it down, investigated it, and found out that the City wanted to transfer the land to the Bay Area Rapid Transit (BART). We had another dog fight on our hands.

We fought like hell to keep our dog park. We incorporated so as to get more clout. We knew we had to stop being just a casual neighborhood group. And we lobbied and lobbied. At the same time, we knew BART and Berkeley hated each other, so we quietly negotiated with BART. At the hearing, ninety of us from the club showed up at the council meeting in teal blue T-shirts with our dog park association name and paw prints on them. In the end, there was a unanimous vote to leave the dog park alone.

The Parks Department installed a monument to me in the park and a plaque for my years of service. A lot of people thought I'd died! It's a genuine fire hydrant painted blue and put next to a tree where chasing dogs won't run into it. People said, "Doesn't she know what they'll do to this?" I think that's funny, and it's fitting.

One day, I was visiting Flagstaff, Arizona, with my friend. We saw a sign for a dog park. It was the first one outside Berkeley I'd ever seen! I thought "Whoa! This is delightful. This has really caught on!" I asked, but they'd never heard of our Berkeley dog park. Now I get calls from all over. I even helped people in Finland get their first dog park. Someone once asked me if I were reborn as a dog, what kind I'd like to be. I think I'd probably be a Sheltie because I like to organize people and make up the rules.

When the Chips Are
Down, Do It Yourself

Rachel Rosenthal is a powerful performance artist and the founder of the Rachel Rosenthal Company. Her performances have a way of dancing around in your head for days after you have seen them, much the way Rachel herself dances on stage. She has appeared at Carnegie Hall and the Lincoln Center as well as on campuses across the United States, and has enraptured audiences from Sydney to Brussels. She leaves those who watch her thinking or rethinking their ideas about human behavior and obligations because her work is so provocative. Her empathy and family experiences (including fleeing the Nazis during World War II) have contributed, no doubt, to her desire to wake up the world, which she has done with a creation of electrifying performances that combine various mediums, including music, words, videos, costumes, paintings, lighting, and dance. In 2000, Rachel delivered her last performance in Wales, before, as she puts it, "throwing in the towel."

At eighty, Rachel still teaches, directs a company, and paints, the latter bringing her life full circle, for she began her creative life "with a continually active pencil/ brush/pen/pastel/chalk between my fingers," drawing fairies, angels, and marquises and designing magic wands. A sometimes quiet, often dramatic, powerhouse of a person, Rachel is impressive for another reason as well: She practices what she preaches. She takes personal responsibility, something she has challenged her audience to do from the stage. I believe her work and her forceful determination are epitomized by this little story of how the "private Rachel" would not take "no" for an answer when something vital needed to be done. This is clear in the story of her rescue of Dibidi, the cat who became her inspiration and an inspirational motif for Rachel's students worldwide.

191

In 1979, I began to feel there was a lot of despair in this world, both individual and collective, that could be assuaged in a different manner than I'd thus far encountered. Therefore, I gathered up every technique, every method, I'd learned or taught myself over the years and melded them all into what I call the D.B.D. (Doing By Doing) Experience. A D.B.D. workshop takes place over a weekend and incorporates body exercises, breathing techniques, communication exercises, vocal experimentation, improvisational dramatics—all of which is nonverbal—alone and with others. What I try to do is separate people from their everyday lives. It's like taking a bath in Lethe, the River of Forgetfulness. And it's done through body movement, relaxation, awareness of letting go, guided imagery, and guided meditations. I work to help people bring consciousness into the body instead of being like a disembodied head and I must say I've seen some magnificent results. And while I hope to inspire others to live fruitful, powerful, and joyful lives, it's truly one precious being who inspired me to reinvigorate and reshape my own life.

When lived in New York, I was given my first kitten whom I called Dibidi. One day Dibidi disappeared. I searched for her all over the streets of Lower Manhattan, and the roofs over and adjacent to the loft where I lived. This went on for three days and nights. On the third day, I was on the roof, where several chimneys had been bricked over in my absence (I didn't dare think that she could have fallen down one of these and been buried alive like in a Poe story) and, leaning on a still-open chimney, I wept, watching my tears falling into the five-story chimney shaft and disappearing within its darkness.

As I tried to focus through my tears, I saw a small, almond-shaped green light way down in the chimney, soon joined by another. I saw her eyes and she spoke to me. I yelled at her in French (because we spoke French to each other) to be patient, and that I would get her out. No one could help because it was Saturday afternoon and even the SPCA [the Society for the Prevention of Cruelty to Animals] never responded. The police came but laughed at me and I threw them out. I calculated visually that she must be at the level of the second floor. I took some tools and broke into the mimeographing store and began to hammer a hole where I thought Dibidi might be, into a bricked-over fireplace, running up to the roof intermittently to remind her to hang on because I was coming. Finally, I had a hole large enough for my head and one arm. I looked inside the chimney, but I had miscalculated by about five feet. I tried to send down a makeshift dumbwaiter, but Dibidi was hanging onto the chimney wall for dear life, because it was the spot where the incline of the shaft became vertical. She was covered with the plaster of my hammering and wouldn't dare let go to jump up on that diminutive elevator.

I knew I should get her up with a noose around her neck but feared of doing it wrong and either killing her or dropping her back into the depth of the remaining chimney shaft. I got up my courage, made a noose, got it around her neck after a few tries, and hauled her up. I grabbed her and ran up to my loft where I had food and drink waiting. But Dibidi didn't eat or drink until she had truly thanked me, with her backside up and her head on the floor. This she did several times, falling over in her weak state, keeping me within her vision. I couldn't hold and squeeze her enough as she purred and purred. Her rescue had taken five hours.

But that was not the end of the Dibidi saga. One morning, after we had moved to California, I heard scratching under the cantilevered part of the house and realized in a flash that Dibidi, awakened from sleep on the porch by a passing dog, had made the mistake of climbing a trellis instead of jumping inside through the open window. She hung onto the underside of the cantilever as long as she could, with the dog below. I was down the steps and in the street in one jump just as Dibidi fell, hitting some rocks at the bottom and breaking her back. We raced to the vets, a white hankie tied to the side mirror, announcing to the traffic that this was an emergency. Dibidi was in shock, between life and death. Soon she was out of shock and into a body cast within which she had to be turned from side to side every two hours, night and day. The vet said she might have six months to live: "Cats can't live without any leg mobility."

Dibidi lived another twelve years and died at age eighteen. She had me where she wanted me: as her constant and perpetual slave. We went everywhere together, including New York, San Francisco, Big Sur, etc. When her cast came off and it was obvious that she was a paraplegic, she learned to do her business over the toilet, lying on my knee after I raised her tail. She went through the Laurel Canyon fire of 1959, the earthquake of 1971, and countless storms and adventures, with our connection growing with the years. I ran with her, one hand under her belly, following where she wanted to go, I helped her jump on beds, chairs, and sofas, and she developed strong chest muscles to pull herself forward when I wasn't holding her up.

Dibidi taught me the most important lesson in life: how to live with limitations. She did everything in spite of becoming a paraplegic! During the years she was a paraplegic, I was developing acute degenerative arthritis in my knees. Inspired by her bravery, I continued to perform and live an active life in spite of my near-infirmity, just as she did. It is because of her that I have been able to teach so many people the importance of individual action, the beauty of loving relationships, and most of all, the importance of "Doing By Doing," or D.B.D., the esoteric meaning of Dibidi's name. And when I tell Dibidi's story in my workshops, people always cry because this little cat's soul and her perseverance touches them like nothing else. They leave with the image of Dibidi to help them through their lives.

Everyone Needs to Eat

Margaret River, Australia, is touted as one of the prettiest spots on that continent, which is saying something in a land where spectacular waves crash onto pristine beaches and you can travel through miles of natural beauty that is the Outback. Thousands of visitors journey to Margaret River, and over the years, a growing number of those with enough money to do so have put down roots and put up homes there.

When he left college, Dave Seegar moved from England to Margaret River, a town he loved for its jaw-dropping flora and fauna, its sunshine, and, most particularly, for the birds he loved to study. Margaret River seemed the perfect place to live, a truly friendly community. But then something happened. That "something" was an influx of the rich and the subsequent gentrification of the town. As if overnight, people who had fallen on hard times found themselves unable to afford to live or eat there. They were being forced out of the area where many of them had been born and raised. David saw a need and decided he could do something about it. He founded a "soup kitchen" of sorts where hearty meals would be served, somewhere to eat for those who couldn't keep up with the Joneses, called The Soupie. Today, Dave himself is also known as "the Soupie." His good deed has blossomed from a seed of thought into a magnificent enterprise that serves the community's neediest residents. That sort of idea fits the bill and this book perfectly!

In postwar England, the naval ship-building industry was in sharp decline and many people lost their jobs. So, in 1963, my father, a ship builder, accepted an offer from a company in Calcutta, India, and off we went. My memories of those days are of swimming in the streets during the cooling monsoon rains and feeding monkeys nuts from brown paper bags. Then we went back to England, and I missed all the wildlife and the sun. Luckily, when I married, my wife and I decided to move to Australia, to a beach town called Margaret River, where the trees are full of beautiful birds and the sun shines most of the time. To us it was paradise. We settled down and I started to study the birds that interest me. But in short order, things took a nasty turn.

It happened when a new editor took over our local newspaper. Our town is a fairly unique country town, or it was. It has always been colorful and fairly accepting of differences, all sorts of differences. It's attractive to seasonal workers, backpackers, surfers, and tourists alike, each to his or her own. The new editor, however, didn't like "hippies," he didn't like "ferals" (the wild animals who were here first), he didn't like homeless people, and he didn't like people who weren't able to get a job at the moment—and he was outspoken in expressing his opinions on the newspaper's pages. He thought he knew what was best for this town better than the locals did. A growing number of residents, the newcomers, apparently agreed with him, and tensions began to rise.

I've always been interested in changing things for the better, but I never thought that I actually possessed those intrinsic qualities that affect change. However, as we all know, you can't change something by simply thinking about it, although it would be brilliant if we could! You have to act. So driven by the injustice of this editor's attitude, I decided to do something for the disenfranchised people who were part of our town.

Because it's outrageous that in any wealthy country there are people who have difficulty affording food, let alone good food, I decided to start a local soup kitchen. I had no idea whatsoever if it would be successful, whether it would achieve what I hoped it would achieve, whether anyone would come, or if, indeed, my culinary skills were adequate. I didn't know if I could make a difference, but I had the conviction to try.

I approached the wonderful ladies at the Margaret River Community Resource Centre (MRCRC) about the idea and, luckily, they liked it a lot. The Centre was originally a hospital, so it already had a large kitchen. The MRCRC kindly provided me with what we call a "Groupie," a small weatherboard house with a verandah, to serve from. Later, they provided all my pots and pans and associated utensils. They are totally supportive, fantastic people. With the help of a few friends, I scrounged up the initial funds to buy food and other bits and pieces and, through donations for meals, the funding is largely self-perpetuating. We charge a small amount for the meal and it covers our costs. It was all unbelievably easy, really. You buy produce, you follow a recipe, and you serve it, collect the bill, and clean up!

I didn't have ambitions beyond Margaret River, but it seems that The Soupie, as it is called, has made a big difference, not just here but in other towns as well. Now there are two other soup kitchens operating in Western Australia, both inspired by this one. Perhaps surprisingly, the media has covered the kitchen, including the Discovery Channel, so that may help give an idea to others facing gentrification in their own areas, wherever they are. All in all, it's been great! We have enthusiastic local support, wonderful volunteers, regular customers who love us, and we've made damned good friends.

Contrary to common culinary connections, this soup kitchen has nothing to do with soup, but it has everything to do with healthy, hearty food. We cook curries and pulses [split peas, beans, lentils, and the like], good solid Mexican beans, Louisiana gumbos, Hungarian ratatouille, and much more, all served with brown rice and a great big salad. And all the food is healthy because it's vegan. We charge three dollars for a meal, which consists of huge portions, and any profits we make we donate to other charities so we can also help to make a difference elsewhere as well.

If I could point to one person who illustrates what the Soupie is all about, it might be John Thomas-Connelly. John was a local gentleman who lived here for twelve or thirteen years and was in his forties when I met him. He was very colorful, very polite. When John was twenty-two and on leave from his job as a cook at a mining camp in Perth, he was hit by a tractor-trailer, meaning that in the prime of his life, his body was simply broken apart. He lost both of his legs and died three times on the operating table whilst the surgeons were trying to stabilize him. One day, John turned up on his crutches at the Soupie and offered his services as a volunteer. We welcomed him, as we do all volunteers. John would come in twice a week, sit at the kitchen table with a bag of carrots, or potatoes to peel, and proceed to talk and eat, talk and eat, talk and eat. He had no obvious social life, so his capacity for conversation and social interaction was rapacious. On a busy summer evening, we might get 150–200 customers of all colors, races, and nationalities, and loads of pretty girls, and he'd talk to them all. Everybody loved him, and at the Soupie, he shone.

Perhaps the burden and pain of life was too much for his body to contend with any longer, and, one day, he died in his sleep. At his funeral we provided all the food; most of the members of his funeral procession were the friends he'd made at the Soupie, and his wake afterwards was held, yes, that's right, at the Soupie. John's sister told me that the two years John had served with us were the two best years of his beautiful life. This is the greatest honor I've ever received. A healthy meal isn't simply about healthy food, it's also very much about a healthy environment in which to eat that food. There is a lengthy oration to that effect by Chief Seattle that I love. In it, this great man asks us to look after all others and the Earth. And there's an old Quaker saying that points out that if you witness an injustice being committed but you stand by, look on, and do nothing, then you are as guilty of that injustice as the perpetrators. They both boil down to the same thing.

Plucking Music from Your Heart

An icon of the "peace generation," the Beatles' musical mentor (George Harrison called him "The Godfather of World Music"), and the finest sitar player ever, Ravi Shankar is known as India's musical ambassador, the man who has brought its traditional music to all other lands. And like the very best of ambassadors, he is hugely amicable, bubbling over with fun and enthusiasm. His nature, like his music, can pull the downtrodden up and fill a heart with joy in the darkest of moments.

On a personal level, since the sixties, when my generation sat mesmerized by his work, I have felt great respect for this musical legend. More recently, coming to know his kind and loving wife, Sukanya, and one of his two talented daughters, Anoushka, my affection has grown to encompass the whole family. Anoushka and her father have helped campaign to improve conditions for some of the most blighted animals on earth—the bulls who pull overloaded carts along the dusty streets of India—and they have spoken out against Kentucky Fried Chicken's treatment of the birds who end up in its buckets. His hectic tour schedule was never a reason to refuse a call to compassionate action, and although not everyone is lucky enough to be born with Ravi Shankar's inherent musical ability, his spirituality and work ethic provide lessons for every reader.

grew up on two different continents: India and Europe. I was born in the holy town of Benares and spent my first ten years absorbing the spiritual, religious, traditional, and cultural life that spread along the river Ganga. I would play in the streets (Vishwanath Galli being my favorite), visit the temples of Shiva, Durga, Kali, and Hanuman, and run up and down the "Ghats," which are sloping embankments with tiers of steps down to the river, all of which left a strong influence on my mind and guided my thoughts and beliefs. The Ghats, in particular, moved me. There one can witness the complete cycle of life, from childbirth to death. My greatest joy and excitement as a child was to visit the Ghats with my mother, my brothers, and their friends. There was so much activity and entertainment, and so many different kinds of music. In fact, all of Benares, or Varanasi as it is called now, resonates with sound; it is inescapable and varied. Benares was so cosmopolitan. People came from all over India to this city of pilgrimage. You could hear the *shehnai* [a wind instrument sometimes called India's oboe] being played at the temples, and wonderful ragas carried through the air, conveying to all the mood of a particular hour of the day or night. I also have vivid memories of my mother singing beautiful lullabies to us, and I remember the inviting smell of her cooking; she was so full of love and everything was magical. Still fresh in my memory is my first experience of the cinema, when I was about three. I went with my brother and a few friends to see some kind of jungle adventure film from Hollywood. I don't imagine it could really have been a 3-D film, but there was a scene where the tiger seemed to jump directly out of the screen, scaring the life out of me. I shrieked and they had to carry me home in a great state of agitation!

Contrasted with this is my time in the West. From the age of ten until I was a young man of eighteen, I lived in Paris and, for two of those years, attended a French Catholic school. I rarely saw my father, a busy government minister, but I realized later that he worked extremely hard and was a gifted philosopher. The long journey by ship from Bombay to Paris remains very vivid in my mind, as does the magnificent house in which we lived, and meeting so many famous people who came to pay their respects to my family. I didn't realize then how famous they were, like Gertrude Stein, Henry Miller, Cole Porter, and so on. When I think back, I realize that except for about a year and a half, I had almost no childhood. I grew up very fast being amidst adults all the time. But listening to all the music from Indian classical, folk, and light music, Western classical, folk, and jazz, seeing the greatest of Indian and Western dancers, theatres, films, vaudeville shows, my head was filled with so many great art forms! It helped me a great deal in the later formative and creative years.

I practically grew up onstage. I might have been five or six when I started singing some songs by the great Indian poet and composer Rabindranath Tagore. I was aware of people listening and admiring me, and I felt high for the first time. My eldest brother, Uday, who I called "Dada," was a dancer who introduced Indian dance and music to the West. Once we got to Paris, I started dancing and playing music in his troupe and we trained and rehearsed together in a mansion that was our musical headquarters. Dada presented the first such "exotic" Eastern performance at *Théâtre des Champs-Élysées,* the prestigious Paris theater, and it was a thundering success. It was also my debut onstage, just a week before I turned eleven! The great impresario, Solomon Hurok, witnessed this show and immediately booked us for a U.S. tour starting in December 1932. We had three more tours by Hurok in 1934, 1936, and the last one in early 1938. Then, because of World War II, Dada disbanded the troupe.

Later, when I was touring Europe and then America with Uday, Baba Allauddin Khan, one of the greatest musicians and players of the sarod [a classical wind instrument] in history, joined our troupe for a year. Hearing him play, I felt a surge of music within me. In fact, he was the great influence who changed the whole pattern of my life. I was amazed to see someone so deeply, reverently, and lovingly attached to his music. He started teaching me sitar and singing while we toured Europe, but he always rebuked me for being flippant, calling me a "butterfly" for doing so many things and not being focused on one thing: music. He said, "Come to me if you can leave everything, and I will teach you!" Although I was getting good reviews as a dancer, Baba's words bugged me, so, after returning to India in 1938, I made a beeline to Baba at his place in the remote city of Maihar and asked him to become my guru. No matter how talented you are there is no shortcut to achievement (except a fluke!). Hard work under proper direction is a must. From then on, I performed on the sitar to admiring listeners.

I had wonderful success: I started getting quite popular in India in the mid-forties. From the mid-fifties, I was performing abroad and by the late fifties and early sixties, I started to perform in all the major concert halls of the world. Among the most astonishing experiences was meeting and working with Yehudi Menuhin, the extraordinary violinist who famously performed for Allied troops during WWII, and who became very significant in my life. He was not only a brilliant musician who taught me a great deal about European classical music but a humanitarian, and our collaboration personally and professionally brought much joy to us both. Then, of course, in the period when George Harrison became my student, I was like a pop star! I had to be very careful during all these excitements, not to compromise my music.

I look upon myself as a crusader, working to bring the music of my country to all the people of the world, something that started in my youth when I saw the way audiences in the West received my music. Spreading that feeling has been a great motivation for me. When I close my eyes and play, I feel I reach such heights and also a world with peace and a state of mind when nothing matters. It's like being united with the ultimate guest—God. Everyone needs a song in his heart. There is a song ("Hey Nath") that came straight out of my heart that has become my main personal prayer in trying to cleanse my soul! It is in Hindi. The nearest translation would be:

Oh, Lord, be benevolent towards me.
Taking away the darkness, give me the light of wisdom.
Take away jealousy, hatred, greed, and anger from me.
Fill my heart with love and "PEACE!"

Born to Be a Rabble-Rouser

When I first heard "Reverend Al" speak I realized that he was a born orator, a street preacher. I felt he was someone with an interesting story. And I was right. Reverend Al grew up in Brooklyn, where by age four he was known as the "wonder boy preacher." He went on to become a Pentecostal minister, lead student pickets over discrimination, champion voting rights, encourage civil disobedience as a means of change, and tour with his surrogate father, the legendary James Brown. In 1991, an attempted assassin stabbed him in the chest with a knife, permanently damaging his lungs.

Never ducking controversy, he has in later years supported Abner Louima, a Haitian immigrant brutalized by Brooklyn police in 1997; organized protests when New York City police shot an unarmed Amadou Diallo forty-one times in 1999; and, in 2001, spent ninety days in jail for protesting the U.S. Navy's bombing of the Puerto Rican island of Vieques. I asked Reverend Al to contribute an essay because he has never backed down from any cause that touches his heart and such resolve is inspiring.

Growing up, my parents took the family south for Christmas every year to visit my grandparents. These trips were pleasant, but largely uneventful. Then when I was eight or nine I encountered what I call my first outrage. Although I was young, I was already preaching. I'd begun when I was four years old and had been on tour with various gospel groups, including

Mahalia Jackson. I say this because I was a profoundly spiritual child, but even so, this moment had a deep impact on my life. On the way to my grandmother's, we pulled into a restaurant in North Carolina and this little weakling of a guy, a white guy, said, "We don't serve black people here." Now, my father was an amateur boxer: he used to spar with Sugar Ray Robinson. So, I had this image that he was invincible. He owned all these buildings in Brooklyn, yet no one would ever try to rob him 'cause it was known that Al would knock you out! But instead of fighting back, we got back in the car and rode toward Alabama. It was the first time I ever saw my father back down. As he drove, he explained to the children about segregation and racism. I think it was the shock of seeing this champion, this macho man, being emasculated in front of me, his son, that made racism even more repugnant than it would have been if I had experienced it another way.

Not surprisingly, in my preteen years I became totally enthralled with the civil rights movement and the social justice movement. Jesse Jackson, Bill Jones, and later James Brown became my mentors. Because of this, I was raised with a sense of being a minister, being an activist, and making a mark. I never realized I had any power of my own until, over the years, people that I respected like Jesse, like Bill, would sit me down and say, "you've got to understand where you are now in life and interpret it." I know it was never anything I read because I never believe anything the media says, pro or con. I read attacks and glowing pieces with the same kind of distrust, because usually it's motivated by something other than a pure heart. But when people that I respect would say it, I knew I'd created a certain level of influence and a certain level of power and I needed to be careful with it all.

Nevertheless, I've faced a lot of obstacles: I've been stabbed leading a nonviolent protest; I've been indicted; I've been incarcerated on civil rights stuff; I've run for office with no money. Yet, I never had any doubt that it would come out all right when I looked to my spiritual side. I would read the papers in the morning if I was under attack to see how bleak it was. Before I would leave home I'd have my morning prayer; I had not a doubt in my mind that this matter would be solved. I just think you have to know what gear to have your personality in. There is a gospel song that's called "The Battle Is Not Yours," meaning that if you really believe what you're doing, it's for more than just you.

One of my proudest moments was my speech at the Democratic National Convention in 2004. My desire was to bring the movement of social justice back to center stage, twenty years after Reverend Jackson's first run and years after King, to let the American mainstream political world know that we're still here and still going to raise these issues. That's why I spoke way over the limit of time given to me and I went off script, because I was not there for Al Sharpton to become mainstream; I was there to complete my assignment: to make sure that every national election cycle knows they have to deal with social justice issues. What I had learned all through the years culminated at that point.

My message to people hoping to make a change is, first, that they should choose something that they're passionate about. The only way you're going to make something count is if you're willing and ready to do the extra work or make the extra effort. There's no career and no life situation that is going to be stress free and obstacle free. Whatever you choose, there's going to be a side to it you do not like and a side to it that is going to be difficult for you. The only thing that's going to make you persevere enough to make a point beyond that is if it's something you're really passionate about and do no matter what.

If you're looking for the easy life, you're not looking to make a point. If you're going to make a real point, you've got to be willing to take the adversity that comes with that because it's like exercise. If I get on the treadmill and run to a speed that doesn't make me sweat, I might do the time but I really haven't benefited from the exercise. The same thing with making a point in life, it doesn't count until it requires more out of you than what's normal. And most people are not willing to do that, which is why most people never leave a mark in life.

Choose your associates carefully. Choose people who will inspire you to be what it is you're trying to be and will inspire you to be determined and will be honest with you about your faults without being a downer, but will not give you false information; will be honest with you but in a helpful way. And be determined: when everything else fails, determination will win. Perseverance and persistence will win. Will is more important than talent and gifts because if you don't have the will, it doesn't matter what talents you've got, you won't pursue it, you won't use it. Will and purpose and determination are the most important things in life.

Being a positive force for change takes courage, but it's fulfilling. I have lived long enough now where some of my enemies have become cordial, because it was never a personal battle; it's always a battle that is for a higher purpose. The only person you ever have to conquer in life is not your enemy, it's yourself. And once you conquer yourself, your ego, your vanity, your misplaced overestimation—once you conquer yourself, then you can fight for a higher purpose and conquer what it is you're supposed to conquer and realize that's what your life purpose is. Most of us, however, go through life without ever asking ourselves what is my purpose? We define success by what we have, not by what we did. But the only success in life is what you did. Because whatever you have, you could lose, and whatever you have, somebody else could have more. But nobody can take from you what you did.

The Importance of Delivering Respect

Russell Simmons is a terrific motivator and savvy businessman who worked his way up from a misspent youth to become a multimillionaire, a hip-hop baron who has made a fortune from producing TV shows, music videos, and hit records. He's also a deeply spiritual man. I have seen people eat a chicken sandwich in the foyer of his Manhattan office, not realizing that the business mogul they are waiting to meet has stood up to protect these little birds and would never kill or eat a single one. Over the years, I have watched him use his forthright, honest style to persuade others to join him in taking strong positions for the underdog, to help those without power seize it. He owns mansions, sports cars, and property; he can buy almost anything he wants, but his interests are in turning out the vote, empowering youth to succeed, and the belief that everyone is part of one family and should treat each other accordingly.

I remember the first time I was treated with respect by some-one of importance in the business world. I was getting off the plane in Amsterdam to promote Kurtis Blow's record (I was his manager at the time) and hearing the president of the Dutch company call me "Mr. Simmons." I remember thinking that my dad must have been there because nobody ever called me that before. It didn't dawn on me then that I could use that respect to benefit anyone other than Kurtis Blow and myself.

Not long after that, I cofounded Def Jam and began producing hip-hop artists. Because of the nature of the music we were putting out there, we attracted a lot of attention. Unfortunately, back then, I had a major phobia of public speaking. In fact, whenever I was nominated for an award I would always send someone in my place in case I won. Then, when we started Def Comedy Jam I had to come out at the end of the show and say, "Thanks for coming out. Good night and G-d Bless." Somehow after doing that again and again, it slowly sunk in that I could speak to more people than could fit in a boardroom. And, not only that, but people were actually listening to what I had to say. So I began to pay more attention to just what it was I was saying.

Around this time, I began doing yoga, and it has greatly influenced my life. I recognize the goal of yoga practice is to put you in the same space that Muslim, Christian, Buddhist, and many other practices, put you in. I recognize there are as many roads to G-d as there are people. I was raised as a Christian but was not religious. I know Jesus did not come to save or reveal Himself but instead came to help us reveal ourselves. He stayed around to promote miracles, not because the world needed them but to show us our highest potential. So, because his miracles were true, I guess I can be considered a Christian Yogi.

My spiritual path has been a gradual process. My first yoga class, about fourteen years ago, was inspiring. I went to the class because there were so many fine girls there, and when I came out I forgot about the girls, forgot about my business, and everything else and was still. That stillness is what I seek every day. It's a practice of reminding yourself and having respect and appreciation for the truth you already know instinctively.

I have been inspired in particular by the second yoga sutra, "Yoga or union with G-d happens with the sensation of the fluctuation of the mind." In other words, when you get rid of all the bullshit, you find your union with G-d. And once my mind began to clear, I was able to take that respect and power I had begun all those years ago in Amsterdam and finally channel it to help not only myself lead a more peaceful life, but to influence the lives of those around me.

If I could tell anyone what not to do in life, it would be, don't waste it and don't whine, just do! If you think you can't get ahead in your job because there's a glass ceiling holding you back, shatter that glass, brush off the shards, and get on with your vision. Get in touch with your passion. Passion is always a driving force in any success.

The Potholed Road from Shy to Shining

Anita Smith lives in the little village of Orlingbury in Northamptonshire, England, with her husband. Her children are grown up now, but because of a fateful vacation they took in 1992, they have all ended up lending their mother a hand in the work she has started doing for less fortunate families. That "holiday" was to Gambia. At the time, knowing that this tiny country is one of the poorest of African countries—which is saying something on a continent beset with civil wars, desertification, and crop failure—Anita was prepared to see poverty. She even thought to bring along in her luggage some gifts for poor children they might encounter. But the children Anita ended up meeting, and what she discovered about how they live and die, eventually transformed her. I love Anita's story because it shows how, when one person realizes a need, no matter how many thousands of miles away that need may be, he or she can rouse a whole community to share its wealth and talents.

England is usually wet, cold, and miserable at the end of winter—one reason that my husband, my children, and I were looking forward to leaving for an overseas vacation. We had chosen Gambia because it was only a six-hour flight and the brochure said, "Sunshine guaranteed!" We knew it was a very poor country, of course, so we brought along some coloring books and crayons to give to children at the local school. I remember thinking that there would no doubt be children who did not have many privileges in life. How little I knew!

After enjoying the beach and doing touristy things for a few days, my children and I set off to visit a school in Banjul, the capital, but they were all closed for a holiday. Someone suggested we go to the children's ward at the Royal Victoria Hospital, the main government hospital, instead, so off we went.

When we got there, I was devastated: the wards were dirty, the equipment was old and in some cases broken. I remember seeing one little girl called Jayna who had sat in her cot for the best part of six months with no staff having the time to pick her up and cuddle her. The nurse explained that her parents, unable to feed her, had abandoned her, placing a concrete block on top of her legs. She was now paralyzed.

On the bus going back to the airport, I was tormented by the idea that I could fly out of this country and the children would be left with nothing. I called the only person I could think of, the author of the guide book we had brought with us, and told him I needed to help the hospital. He was very nice, but he said that if I thought the Royal Victoria was bad, I should go to the hospital in Bansang, about 200 miles inland. He said "I'm a very hardened man. I've traveled the world. But at Bansang, I cried like a baby when I saw the conditions those children were in." I made up my mind that I had to go back and I had to see Bansang Hospital for myself. "God help my marriage," I thought, not knowing then that my husband and my children would all end up helping in their own ways.

Now please don't think I'm the sort of person who usually jumps in with both feet. Far from it. I'm the shyest person on the earth, although in this case my heart ruled my head. In school, I was the child sitting at the very back of the class, and I would rather have died than raise my hand to answer a question. I wouldn't say "boo" to a goose. In fact, my mother had sent me to Belgium when I was in my teens—to an aunt who didn't speak English—in the hope that I'd have to get over my shyness there, but the experience only made me retreat further into my shell than ever! I don't have any nursing experience or a degree either. I left school at fifteen and started work in a florist's shop. The thought of pushing forward in Gambia made me weak at the knees, but I felt I had to grapple with it. The enormity of what needed to be done terrified me, but I knew in my heart that I had to do something, no matter what.

Two months later, I was in Banjul again, my mother in tow, which was a really foolish move, looking back. Among other things, it was fifty degrees Celsius [122 degrees Fahrenheit], mind-bogglingly hot. This time, I went to the minister of health. I told him that if they could get my mother and me to Bansang, I would see what I could do, that I couldn't promise I could help, but I'd try. To my surprise, the minister arranged transport right away. It took sixteen hours to travel that 200 miles, along a road that had potholes in it big enough to swallow a truck whole. That road has deteriorated since, and now, in places it is totally impassible and you have to take three separate ferries. That first night, my mother and I stayed in a mud hut, the roof of which was infested with rats. We could hear them gnawing and running about and were worried that they would fall through onto us. It was pitch dark, as there was no electricity. We were petrified by the sounds we kept hearing, sometimes sounds like carcasses being dragged around, animal noises. Both of us sat bolt upright much of the time. The next morning, my mother had her things in her case and was at the end of the road at dawn, ready to go back home. I stayed on for four days.

When I entered the hospital, it was beyond bleak. The operating room had a dirty floor and broken windows that allowed

dust to blow in. As far as I could tell, there was virtually nothing in the way of pain relief or other drugs. Ether was the only
anesthetic. The electricity could be off for days, and the nurses
would have to work by candlelight. No electricity also meant
no water, as the water was provided by an electric pump. The
staff is hardworking and dedicated, but despair and a sense of
helplessness was written all over their faces. The sick journeyed
for many miles on foot or by horse cart only to be met by
hopelessness and despair.

Stepping into the children's ward, it took a while for my
eyes to adjust to the darkness. When they did, I saw there were
old beds with pieces of foam contaminated with every imaginable body fluid and up to four children sharing a bed. Mothers
slept under the bed, at the sides of the beds, and in the corri-
dors. As a mother, my heart broke. My first reaction was one of
stunned horror and a feeling of helplessness. It was awful to see
children in these conditions for no reason other than they were
poor. You don't have to speak the language to be able to communicate. You only have to look into another mother's eyes to
know her feelings.

Some of the children had dysentery, and the stench of the
place was so strong that it took all my strength to suppress
my desire to heave. There were no bandages, just strips of rags
holding drips to tiny arms. I learned that an incredible number of children die in infancy and that one in four children in
Gambia don't survive to see their fifth birthday. I had brought
toys with me, but the children had never had a toy, so at first
they had no idea what they were. They didn't pick them up.
That was my introduction to Bansang.

Before I left the area, I had an experience that moved me
greatly and hardened my resolve. A child had been propped up
opposite me on a wooden bench in the back of a jeep going to
the hospital. He had a horribly deformed face and I found that

I simply couldn't muster the courage to look at him and smile, although I knew he was staring at me all the time. I was feeling too emotional to look at him, afraid I would break down and that he would see me cry. But when we got to the hospital, he was too weak to walk, so I had to pick him up and carry him inside. His frame was skeletal. When I went to leave him, I looked at his face and saw that he was terrified, absolutely terrified. I left him some clean clothes and a washcloth, but he died the next day. He was one of the first children I saw die.

As soon as I got back to the U.K., I knew I had to give talks about Bansang to raise support and money to buy vital drugs and supplies, but I shook with fear. Once, getting ready to address a meeting, I was so tense that a glass I was holding actually shattered in my hand. Eventually I got a prescription for beta blockers to calm my nerves and that has helped, but what kept me going early on was the memory of that child I had carried into the hospital who had died.

I asked everyone to help, including my doctor, Dr. Peter McCormick. He said no, he couldn't, he was retiring and, after all, he was a general practitioner and didn't know anything about diseases like malaria and snakebite, so he wouldn't be any use. But, incredibly, that night, he called me at home. He said he'd been thinking about what I had said and had decided to go to the Liverpool School of Tropical Medicine to learn what he needed to know! Dr. McCormick ended up being a literal lifesaver. He not only has spent time as a volunteer but has set up practices that continue to save lives to this day. If one person's actions can inspire another, then one need look no further than Peter McCormick, whose connection with Bansang led him to devote the rest of his retirement to helping child cancer patients in Cameroon. I may have inspired him initially, but he has been my mentor and my inspiration. His medical knowledge and his input have kept me going all of these years.

Since those days, Bansang hospital has changed from a place of despair and helplessness to a place of healing and hope. Thanks to the love, compassion, and generosity of so many people from all walks of life, the child patients are no longer treated in a dark, dank ward. We have just completed a purpose-built eighty-bed children's unit, and mortality rates have been reduced by a staggering 73 percent.

I go back several times a year to oversee ongoing building projects. My long-term aim is to bring the rest of the hospital up to the standards of the children's unit, as every patient deserves to be treated with dignity and compassion.

It is true to say that my life is far richer now than ever before. You cannot do better than to see a child smile and say "thank you" when all you have done is try to make him a little more comfortable. My heart goes out to the deeply caring staff that give their all in Gambia, resisting the urge to flee to better prospects in the West.

One day after returning from Gambia, I picked up my mail and found in it a tattered letter. The letter was from an illiterate and very poor man who had traveled at great cost back to the hospital from his village to see me. Finding I was not there, he asked for my address and then engaged someone to write to me. The letter simply said "Thank you for loving my son."

What greater tribute can anyone want in life?

Guided by Ghosts

Oliver Stone has won five Golden Globes and three Academy Awards for his films (Platoon, Born on the 4th of July, *and* Midnight Express*), and has been nominated almost too many times for too many different awards to count. Parts of his first book,* A Child's Night Dream, *ended up in the East River when its author, consumed with anguish over his experiences, threw them into the water, together with certificates for his Purple Heart and Bronze Star for "extraordinary acts of courage under fire," the medals he won in combat in Vietnam. Always controversial—for when is there a time when strong political views are not the subject of angry debate?—Oliver Stone has rocked complacency with his challenges to, among other things, the official story that "explains" the death of President John F. Kennedy. He's also exposed many a raw nerve with his autobiographical and semiautobiographical portrayal of war and its effects.*

Oliver Stone's mother taught him to be kind to animals: he was one of the first to sign a petition asking NASA to stop sending monkeys into space, a campaign PETA eventually won. Caged animals even appear as metaphors for his mentally anguished self in his earliest film work, Last Year in Vietnam, *a portrayal of his life as a returned (wounded) veteran who is tormented by what he has seen of war and is trying to make sense of his life. He is a powerful bear of a man who belongs in this book because he will be damned if he'll let history slide away unnoticed.*

grew up believing in service to my country, and that if we go to war we go to war together. On top of which, I felt strongly, and still do, that ignoring your obligations is wrong. So when the Vietnam War began, I went. I believed what we were being told by the government and the press. I believed in a communist threat. It took me several years to wake up. Not that I came back a protestor: I didn't. I came back neutral and alienated, wounded inside and out, tormented by all I'd seen: the carnage, the misery, the suffering, and the aggression of the human race.

I was in the Twenty-Fifth Infantry Division and First Cavalry Division, and saw quite a bit of combat in the ground war during 1967 and 1968. I wasn't at the My Lai massacre, but I saw that kind of behavior. Our mission had become distorted, reduced to a survival course. What with the beginning of race issues, and small-scale mutinies, where enlisted men were refusing to take orders from the officers, and the drugs, everything was starting to go wrong. What can I say? Vietnam is a state of mind, what happened there is still going on somewhere else. This both frustrates and saddens me. People now are too young to remember the damage of that war and haven't elected to study it, or those old enough to remember, don't. It could have been a war that brought about a collective shift in perspective, but instead, in the nineties, you could see the march to war beginning all over again. The war in Iraq is a totally logical result of our aggression mentality turned outward.

When I got back, there was little support for veterans. Very few had heard of posttraumatic stress disorder. I was very lucky to be reintegrated back into society, to find my first wife, to get an education. Lots of soldiers didn't make it back at all or never found their way after they did. I landed in New York and enrolled in film school. It wasn't a knowingly pivotal decision, but some friends encouraged me. I'd always liked movies as a kid, and the GI Bill offered a subsidy and New York University was close to home, so off I went. I couldn't believe someone was going to pay me to watch movies! It took time to learn the process of making a film: I started out writing many screenplays that were never produced, held other jobs, but I knew from the strong reactions I got, pro and con, to my book *Last Year in Vietnam* that I could make something important for the screen. *Platoon* is semiautobiographical, and when veterans saw it, many were deeply moved. Here was someone from the ranks willing to tell the story straight, from the ground point of view. This was not the same war story we were officially hearing. I felt in 1986, when the film came out, it was a great moment for America, that we were ready to move beyond what we were being fed, ready to get to the raw truth of it all, somewhat like what's going on finally in Iraq.

There's a tendency to denature and sanitize things and to come up with the easily digestible answer, a sort of virtual reality. Hitler said, "the bigger the lie, the more people will believe it," and, sadly, he was right. The danger is in becoming a nation of sheep, each of us a rubberstamp, a cipher, an unengaged and unthinking person rather than a participant in the democratic process. But real democracy is about listening to all the arguments, learning to think for ourselves, and resisting being spoon-fed by the politicians and the press. That's the Socratic method. I can't think of anything that is more important than the pursuit of truth, even if you have to wade through blood and dirt to get to it, even if pursuing it requires sacrifice and effort. It's my hope that my films help.

All life is change, but we're destined to repeat history if we don't study the past, especially our history of war. Some people think we should let the ghosts rest and that we shouldn't show the blood and guts of reality, but I disagree. Everyone who watches films such as mine is strong enough to take something from the bad energy as well as the good. As for ghosts, I believe in them: they have important stories to tell if we'll just listen.

Keeping Presidents Honest

I first heard Helen Thomas speak at the memorial service for a mutual friend, her contemporary, the humanitarian reporter Ann Cottrell Free. Like Ann's, Helen's career has spanned the Great Depression and taken her into the White House. Both women cared about the poor, the oppressed, about fair play, and democracy, both took no prisoners when pursuing a story. Helen Thomas is called "The First Lady of the Press," and known for her sharp, probing questions, ones she has asked of every president since John F. Kennedy as well as of their press secretaries. For forty-six years she has sat in the front row at all White House news conferences, and until the current Bush administration broke with tradition, had always spoken the last words, "Thank you, Mr. President." A servant of the truth with a probing questioning style President Ford described as "acupuncture," she is fond of saying that the shortest distance between two points is a straight line. Her views on how to make a difference in life suit this book perfectly.

When I was a sophomore in high school, we had to write something for English class about news reporting. I can't remember what it was, but my report got into the school paper. I saw my byline and said, "This is for me!" In my view, I'd arrived. I knew that if I chose reporting as a career, I'd have the kind of life that would allow me to indulge my curiosity, keep me learning my whole life through. There would be work before me every day because something happens every day. Reporting would allow me a sense of independence while I was out there getting the story, and it would satisfy my drive to achieve something good. I'd found what I wanted to do. I'd recommend that to anyone: do what will make you happy in life, happy at work, because if you aren't happy, you're not in good shape.

Having been bitten by the reporting bug, I took it with me to Wayne State University. There were no real journalism classes then, but I loved English and I loved history and that's what I needed for my job. Since that time, I've covered history every day. I wasn't the first woman reporter, women have been in the newspaper business for 150 years, but, nevertheless, when I began it was very much a man's world. Women were encouraged to be teachers and nurses, as those were considered secure jobs. Barriers to us were up all over the place. Women couldn't belong to press clubs, for instance. Those barriers had to be overcome and eventually they were, but not without great passion and effort. Suffragettes chained themselves to the White House fence, were arrested, carried off; there was a struggle for women to get the vote. There will always be struggles.

I've had disappointments in my time, of course. If you're never disappointed, you're not alive! But I never let things get me down; you can't expect life to be a smooth run. What's important is not to let setbacks keep you from moving ahead. If you're persistent and never deviate from your path, and if you're in the right, meaning you're doing something legal and moral, you'll be okay. Speaking the truth is my Gold Standard. Unless you're blocked by a secretive government, you can always seek and find the truth, and you must never stop trying to get it.

I've been so lucky to pick a profession where I get educated every day. News is news and as long as there are people on this planet, there will be an interest in what's going on. To report honestly is a public service, I can contribute something, inform people. A healthy democracy requires an informed people, facts make a country safe, and facts protect people. The questions I ask aren't just my questions, they're the people's questions. As a member of the press, I carry a responsibility to ask them. Since becoming a reporter, I've been to nine inaugurations, all of them moments of great hope. All presidents mean well as they come to office, but then a funny thing happens on the way to the forum.

Nevertheless, I firmly believe that democracy works. For instance, President Kennedy's assassination was the most traumatic event in my career and could have resulted in a time of great political upheaval. Yet, the transition to President Lyndon Johnson was very smooth; he stepped into office immediately. There was no coup d'etat, our government simply went on about its business. However, democracy isn't working so well in this administration. We have a president who can't explain this war in Iraq. He can't give a valid reason for it, and that's so shocking. Thousands of lives are being lost. We're killing people who did nothing to us. We raise young people to do the right thing, not to lie and cheat and steal and kill and then we all of a sudden tell them to go kill people who've done nothing to them. I stew about this every day.

If there are words I've carried with me through my life they belong to a sports writer who came to my high school. After his talk, we went up to him to get his autograph. He said no, he wouldn't sign any autographs. He said, "Never ask for such a thing. You are as good as anyone else." When a press secretary avoids a question or isn't behaving as he should, I remember those words. I remind him that he's a public servant, that we're paying him, that he's not there to do us a favor, he owes us an explanation, an accounting. People should understand: we don't have a king or a dictator. A president can be impeached if he does something wrong. Being a citizen gives you rights you must never forget you have. Rights that are secured in the Bill of Rights. Let this fact give you strength, don't let people push you around, and always do the right thing.

The Strongest of Victims

There is a very personal reason that Cheryl Ward-Kaiser sits on the California Juvenile Justice Commission, speaks to youth in detention centers, campaigns for political candidates who will forward the rights of victims of crimes, and supports the Justice and Reconciliation project. One night, five young people broke into her bedroom and woke her up not only out of sleep but out of any sense of security she might have had. She witnessed her daughter being raped and her husband's murder.

Since that time, Cheryl has worked hard to forgive the perpetrators, all of whom were identified and arrested and are serving or have served time in jail. She asked to and did meet the driver of the getaway car and the man who kept his foot on her back that night. She not only believes that victims have the right to question those who have interrupted their lives, but also feels strongly that she has something to offer that may affect or prevent future crimes. If anyone belongs in this book, it is a person who works to stop violence, and I believe that Cheryl does just that.

I no longer live in a fluffy world. I'm a serious person. I might enjoy talking about my wonderful grandchildren, say, or the wonderful man I married years after the crime (the arresting officer on my case). But, I live in the real world now, a world where we must work to reach youngsters, even those who've already offended, and prevent more horrible things from happening out there. I was shocked to find out how young the perpetrators were in the attack on my family. Lying there on the floor with a shotgun to my head, I'd guessed that they were in their late twenties, but they were actually only eighteen, nineteen, and twenty. The girl who drove the getaway car was all of sixteen! I found out later that they had committed seventeen other robberies before then.

When they burst into the room, my husband, Jamie, and I didn't have time to get out of bed. The noise went from zero to 1,000 in a second. One of the men forced me to the ground with his foot on my back. They cursed the whole time as they dragged Jamie on his knees from place to place, searching for the safe they were convinced we had but didn't. They found an envelope of cash that Jamie was going to use to surprise me the next day by buying a soft water heater I'd wanted for thirteen years! They started counting it out and they couldn't even count it right. I heard the man's hand hitting my rosary on the trunk near my bed as he rifled through the money. Then, they pulled my seventeen-year-old daughter, Roxie, into the room, made her strip, and raped her with the barrel of a gun in front of her dad. What I couldn't see, I could hear.

As strange as it may sound, I never felt afraid, although I was convinced I was going to die. I first prayed to God for forgiveness of my sins and for strength, and then I begged the men not to hurt Roxie. They had such power lust, such a thirst for blood, they were like leeches. As events escalated, the two main criminals got higher and higher on the violence. These men were much bigger than my husband, but he fought so hard that, in the end, they were amazed. I don't think they'd had dads around and didn't know that when you threaten to kill a man's wife and daughter, you may push that man over the edge. They ended up shooting him in the back. After that, the men fled and soon sheriff's officers filled the house.

I was never in shock unless you count the shock of discovering the real world, a world of shit, a world in which a criminal taps you on the shoulder and says, "You're it!" I didn't shed a tear and neither did Roxie, until, many hours later, I got into the shower. Then I broke down. I'd been so protected by marriage. I'd never graduated college, I hadn't worked a paying job in twenty-six years (I was volunteering as a youth counselor, working primarily with pregnant girls when the crime occurred), and we didn't have a lot of savings or a fat insurance policy. I sat on the bed, thinking "I'm now the breadwinner. I'm going to lose this house. I will have to pull Roxie out of private school. I wonder if I can get a job to support myself." As it turned out, Tanimura and Antle, the produce company my husband worked for, were wonderful. They created a job for me, paid me my husband's salary, and told me to go out into the community and make someone's life better to help balance what happened. And that's what I've been trying to do.

The trial lasted twenty-two months. I was excluded from the courtroom most of the time; first because I was a witness, second because the prosecutor was afraid that the offenders' lawyers might win an appeal by arguing that I was such a strong victim that the jury could only convict, and third when I hugged the shooter's mom. Staying outside was torture. I'd lost my husband, my daughter had been raped, my life was upside down. I wanted to see and hear the five on trial and I wanted them to see and hear me.

Finally I was given a chance. California was the first state to pass Proposition 115, the Crime Victims' Justice Reform Act. That law gives victims a voice in the proceedings, and that's a very powerful part of the healing process. I was entitled to address the court at the end in a "victim impact statement," and I did. I spoke from the heart, without notes. I was able to say what I felt and what I wanted. I laid out the facts of my own childhood abuse (I'd been physically abused by my father and sexually abused by my grandfather) because I didn't want the men to use their own childhoods as an excuse. I said, "This is what happened to me, but I made a choice not to grow up to hurt other people. You had the same choice." When it came to sentencing the man who raped my daughter with the shotgun, and who had loved hurting her, I fought against the lighter sentence that was being considered for him. Three times the judge suggested to the lawyers that he would give him twenty-five years to life with the possibility of parole, but I continued to petition for a life sentence without the possibility of parole. They listened, and that's what he got. I felt that he and the shooter would do it again if they ever had the chance.

After the trial, I learned about restorative justice, the concept of bringing victims and offenders together with the goal of accountability and forgiveness. I found this very exciting. So many people, usually those who've not been a victim, talk about verdicts bringing closure. Nothing could be further from the truth. From the moment a crime takes place, it's the beginning of a whole new life. The key is what you do with what has happened to you. I wanted to meet my violators for several reasons. First, I wanted to tell them that I do not hate them and that I forgive them. I wanted to tell them that face to face. Second, because I had so many questions. Why did they choose my house? for instance. My closet was hidden, no one could see it in the dark, and yet the men who entered my bedroom went straight for it. They knew where it was. How? And why did they think my house had a safe? It seems to me someone must have fed them false information. Who would do such a thing still nags me. Third, because I wanted to be sure that they heard everything that they had taken from me and from Roxie and be forced to think about it. I didn't feel vindictive; rather, the only way any of us could begin to heal was by being honest about what had occurred.

I wrote letters to all the prisoners asking if they would let me visit them. The first one I met with, seven years after the crime, was the girl who drove the getaway car. With the help of a mediator, I explained to her what that night had been like for my daughter and me, and what our lives had been like ever since. She hadn't been in the room. She needed to know what she'd been a part of. Then I asked her to repeat everything I'd said back to me. I was able to ask her my questions, but she said she didn't know the answers to most of them. I knew she was lying. Some people think victims will be conned if they talk to prisoners, but I don't think this is the case. A liar is easy to spot inside or out.

Next I met with John, the man who'd held the shotgun to my head. It was extremely moving. I knew he was sorry. I knew he was sorry as it was happening. I shared with him my experience of that evening and he cried. I told him, "Lying on the floor, I named you 'The Nice One,' because you tried to calm the others down, because you kept telling them not to rape my daughter." He couldn't stop crying. We've remained in touch ever since, and I've promised him that I will work for his rehabilitation and support his release. There's no way for those who commit crimes to realize the full impact they've had, the disruption in lives they've caused, all that they've destroyed, unless their victims can tell them and make them confront what they've done. They need to know the rest of the story. To hear it all, to go over it all again, to answer questions, to look at their victims as individuals. Then they, too, get a chance to heal and change. I don't believe in monsters, but in human beings who do monstrous things. I also believe in consequences, not vengeance; I believe in the ability for people to change.

In the beginning, people who were counseling in juvenile detention centers and prisons didn't want real victims to talk to the incarcerated. They thought it would be too traumatic for us or that we'd end up suing the corrections system. My outlook is, "You may feel bad seeing us cry, but we need to, it's good for us to cry!" You can turn something bad into something good and help these kids, who are going to offend again if you don't reach them and teach them empathy. In a classroom setting, kids can be cocky little jackasses. In jail, they get it, there's no more baloney. The response to the speakers' program is terrific. They know that if a victim comes to talk to them, that victim has to care about them. No one is paying the victim, not even gas money, and yet here he or she is. Often no one else has ever cared about these kids, and their crimes have come from hate. Unable to attack the person they hate, perhaps an absent father, they attack someone they don't even know. One of the biggest problems our society has is that there are no fathers out there. I ask an audience of hundreds of incarcerated kids "How many of you have an okay father?" Not a perfect, wonderful father, just an okay father. And less than five will raise their hands. As for adult-offending men, they've been devalued, told they're not necessary.

Cops can't stop crime; they come in afterward to pick up the pieces. Gun control can't stop crime; the criminals will find another way to cause harm. We can only stop crime if we try to understand the roots of the problem and to engage kids before it's too late. I found a saying on one of those cardboard coffee holders. It reads, "I wonder if young people were actively engaged in all aspects of society and thought of themselves as community leaders, problem solvers, role models, mentors and key 'shareholders,' how would the world change? I wonder too.

Building Tribal Dreams

These days, Robert Young can be found living in Bozeman, Montana, where he has bought a home and, together with his wife, Anita, is raising their daughter, Skylar. It's a long way from the gray bustle of Seattle, where he used to live and run a business. He can look out at the mountains now and, instead of traffic, hear the sounds of animals and the wind. It's not just the scenery around him but his vision of the world and his place in it that have changed.

In the late nineties, Robert cofounded Red Feather Development Group, a not-for-profit organization that partners with American Indian communities throughout the western United States to find long-term, sustainable solutions to the housing crisis facing many of their reservations. Red Feather also teaches home maintenance and low-impact, edible landscaping techniques. He surprised the heck out of friends and family when he shut the doors on his former life, but more strikingly, he surprised himself as well. Robert's story isn't just about how he has changed the lives of Native Americans who need housing, it's about how personal change can happen to people who aren't expecting it or looking for it, as long as they don't hang back when opportunity knocks or a new revelation comes their way. That fits perfectly with the idea behind this book.

Looking back, I was your typical, hard-driven business-man. I ran a sportswear company in Seattle and my life was focused on the Great American Dream: house on the hill, cars, vacations, the good life for my family and me. When it came to charity, I had blinders on. I might put change in a cup somewhere but, if I thought anything about charity, I thought that people who "asked for a handout" had probably brought their circumstances upon them themselves, or that the government took care of what really needed to be done. I was beyond naïve!

I was in a restaurant in Taos, New Mexico, having breakfast with a customer, when I saw a little newspaper called *Indian Country Today*. I leafed through it and came across a headline that read: "Several More Elderly People Froze to Death in Their Homes on the Reservation." I found it incredible. What was going on? Who were these people? Why were they freezing? If this was true, why wasn't it on CNN or in my "regular" paper? Surely, the government makes sure such things don't happen. I took the article with me, and it played on my mind.

Coincidentally, at the same time, I started reading the book *Revolution of the Heart* by Bill Shore, which is about a man who, on his way to his Washington, D.C., office, reads an article about tens of thousands of people starving to death in Africa and simply flips the page, something most of us do. When he gets to his office, it occurs to him that once you know something is wrong, you have an obligation to try, at least, to do something about it, even if that something is small. I knew he was right. I shouldn't just ignore the plight of elderly Indians who were freezing to death, now that I knew about it and had resources. I could at least look into it, I thought, maybe link up with some existing organization, and give some money. But, look as I might, I couldn't find anyone who was helping.

I had no interest in becoming a martyr to a cause, throwing myself body and soul into charity work, but after talking things over with my wife and my business associates, I ended up going to the Reservation to have a look for myself. What I saw was a total eye-opener, and what I learned changed me forever. Here were proud people who had been devastated long ago by our government and had never recovered. I met people whose great-grandparents had been killed by the U.S. Army, who had been banned from performing their rituals, had lost their language, their land, everything. They couldn't get jobs, and they were looked down upon by many people outside the Reservation who had no idea of their hardships, how their ancestors had often refused to submit to white rule and had been slaughtered for it. I learned things that aren't in the history books in our schools about the lives of people who had, up until then, been invisible to me. A friend of mine from South Dakota had Indian kids in their high school, but they came off the Reservation for class and went back on afterward. They had known nothing of their experience, yet there was Third World poverty right in their backyard.

The first person I was introduced to on the reservation was Katherine Red Feather, a seventy-five-year-old Lakota grandmother. When I first met her, she was living in a dilapidated trailer, not a mobile home but the kind of trailer you tow behind a car. The wheels had been removed and it sat up on blocks. She had no running water, only an outhouse dug out back. Although Indians are used to people coming onto the Reservation like some "Great White Hope," peddling religion or forcing their ways on the people, Katherine was always kind to me. She helped me understand the reservation and Lakota people; she introduced me to her family, to others in the community, taught me about customs, traditions, so much. Gradually, people learned to trust that I didn't want anything. I didn't come with any strings attached. After that first meeting, twelve years ago, I left thinking, "Let's see what we can do!"

I went back to Seattle, talked to my friends to try to get donations and offers of help lined up. I also asked a Peace Corps friend of mine for her advice, because I knew that she had a big heart. Right off the bat, she introduced me to Stone Gossard, from the band Pearl Jam, and he turned out to be a fantastic, decent, caring individual. He not only offered his financial assistance, but also agreed to travel to South Dakota to help build Katherine's home. Since that time, Stone and Pearl Jam have held a number of concerts that benefited Red Feather Development Group, and he participated on Red Feather's board of directors for over ten years. Stone and Pearl Jam's involvement early on gave us credibility and made an enormous difference.

Our first house was built for Katherine. She came every day to excitedly watch this ragtag group of volunteers camping next to her trailer, struggling to get it done. There were a dozen or so of us, most of us absolutely ignorant of anything to do with building. We picked a two-week period in July, thinking we wouldn't be hampered by rain and, boy, were we wrong! It was not only as hot as a furnace out there, but we experienced torrential rain, massive thunderstorms, and lightning strikes that were about as frightening as you can get. We were lucky to make it out of there alive!

The house was a kit home that arrived in a container and was sold to us at cost by Miles Homes, a company that's out of business now. Katherine moved into her house the very day we finished it and has been there ever since.

During the construction of several homes, we had the honor of being given "a sweat." I learned that Indians were banned from holding sweat lodges for many years during the time of devastation, yet these rituals are integral to many of the tribes, for health as well as for spiritual reasons. The lodges I have gone to have hot rocks placed in a pit in them, and then water is thrown onto the rocks. I can't describe the sheer physical pleasure of being able to enter and cleanse yourself in this way after a day of hard, manual labor. It is an incredible experience. And the fact that it is given to our workers as part of a relationship, as a sign of appreciation, without any preaching of any kind, is so refreshing, it makes me so grateful in return. Each person who has come to build leaves as an ambassador, determined to promote the understanding that nothing is done for people, it is done with people.

Some time after we built our first kit home, we learned to make houses out of straw. It's great, it's organic, it's renewable, and a lot of reservations grow wheat so it's also readily available. We cover the bale walls with lath and stucco, which hardens overnight. Stacking the bale walls is a lot like adult Legos! Big building blocks of straw. It took a long time and a lot of collaboration with Washington University and others to get things right, because the houses must be made to code. If they meet code, then the U.S. government has an obligation to hook up running water, electricity, and other basic amenities. It might take them five years, but they do. Every year our "organization" increases. Since we began, Red Feather's staff and volunteers have finished more than fifty housing-based projects, building homes from scratch, rehabilitating crumbling structures, and even building wheelchair ramps for tribal elders and the disabled.

No one should think that I just jumped into this. My transition was slow. I talked things over with my wife, Anita, and we knew we couldn't do one house and then walk away. In fact, it went from one house to going back with a group of great volunteers every summer, and took me five or six years to move into this full time. I get upset if someone thinks it's all up to others, the way I used to think. It isn't. It's up to each of us to do what we can do to contribute, to ease others' difficulties. Each of us is needed. There is nothing special about me or what I have done. Anyone can do it, anyone at all.

Verses with Purpose

Benjamin Zephaniah is a British Rastafarian novelist, playwright, and dub poet (spoken word over reggae rhythms) whose work is strongly influenced by the music and poetry of Jamaica. He finished school at thirteen and published his first book of poems by twenty-two. He's met with great international acclaim and is beloved by adults and children alike. He defines himself as an oral poet, inspired by the actual sound of words in addition to their meaning. In a time when the Western world views oral traditions as a relic, Zephaniah encourages folks to slow down and listen to the language. He fearlessly uses his writing to tackle political and social concerns. His poems are about racism, misogyny, animal rights, peace (he thinks armies should be banned), and the safety of our environment and he uses humor and plain speak to get his points across.

He has recorded an album with The Wailers, their first since the death of Bob Marley, and hosted Nelson Mandela's Two Nations Concert at the Royal Albert Hall. In 2003, he publicly (typically, if rejected, it's done privately) rejected the honor of becoming an Officer of the Order of the British Empire from the Queen in protest of British government policies, including the decision to go to war in Iraq. He is the only Rastafarian poet to be short-listed for the poetry chairs for both Oxford and Cambridge University.

I chose Benjamin because he is always forthright and because he has had an enormously positive influence on so many people, particularly children. He encourages them to think for themselves, be true to their own ideas, have great fun being the individuals they are, and to never be afraid to be picked on as the odd one out.

From about the age of seven, I had a really strong vision of what I wanted to do and it's exactly what I'm doing now. It was that vivid in my mind. The strange thing was that all the signs were saying, no, you can't do that. A young black guy was always being told you must be a car mechanic, or a painter and decorator, or you must do one of these manual jobs that our parents did driving buses and things like this. And I thought no, I want to write poetry, but I want to write poetry that people identify with. I don't want to write poetry that is pretentious. I want to write poetry that's political and I also want to put poetry into theater and music. And I'd go on like that. And people would say, go on, don't be stupid.

I remember one day my mother said to me, "Look, son, we are guests in this country and we work hard driving buses and being nurses and things like this and you should start thinking of an apprenticeship. You're a black man in a white person's country and you want to be a writer? Now you tell me what person do you know that earns a living from writing?" And I went "Hmmm. . .Shakespeare." And she said, "He's been dead a long time! And that's what will happen to you, you will die too!" She was trying to protect me really, and she was trying to say where are your examples? And I didn't have any examples. What I wanted was in a little world of my own.

I attended school in England in the late sixties. I was the only black child and so I was really, really bullied a lot. There was no sense of racism or prejudice, it was just the norm; it was a Church of England school and I was different and strange. I remember once telling a teacher that some people beat me up and were laughing at me because I was black and the teacher also just laughed at me because I was black. I don't think England was like the States. I think there was a lot of talk about color prejudice, because our parents were invited over from the Caribbean to work at the jobs that white people wouldn't do.

Clean the streets, work in hospitals, and things like this. There were lots of signs; the common sign that any black person of that generation will tell you they saw in those days was a sign that said, "No blacks. No Irish. No dogs." It was in the public houses, the bars. Sometimes you'd go to try to rent a room, an apartment, and the sign would be there.

One of my first experiences with this was walking to my friend's home after school, I was about seven or eight, and his sister met us halfway and said, "you can't bring him into the house because Daddy's at home." So I said, "Oh, that's fine, I'd like to meet your father." So she said, "No, Daddy thinks that all black people should be slaves." So I said, "What are slaves?" I was an innocent boy, you had to explain to me what a slave was. This boy explained it to me in very crude language: "slaves, that was when all black people worked for all white people." I went home to my mother and I said, "Mom, Robert said that black people a long time ago were slaves and that his father thinks we should still be slaves. Is that true?" And my mother said, "Well, you see what happened, son, was, a long time ago black people sinned against God so God repaid us by making us slaves. So don't worry because it may be bad here but when we get to heaven it will be okay." And I remember saying, "Mother, I'm not going to wait to go to heaven to get liberation, no way!" And I managed to live out my vision. The thing that I really feel now that I've come on this journey—although it's always been with me—is that what I had to do was more important than just me. It had to be for other people.

At ten, I gave my first public performance in church, and by fifteen I had a pretty strong following in my hometown amongst the African-Caribbean and Asian community. I was thrilled, but even at that age I knew I wanted to reach more people, I wanted to reach outside of the black community. So in 1979, I headed to London. Getting noticed by the public was very gradual for me. I remember around 1982–83 people writing about me and saying, he's important 'cause of all the things he talks about. I would say things that I thought were pretty average and then it would be quoted in the newspaper the next day and I couldn't believe it was that important! Over the years, I realized that it's not just about me. There's a lot of work to be done. Back then, the first thing I set out to do was popularize poetry. The dead image that academia presented of poetry frustrated me. I wanted people who didn't read books, those who couldn't read books, and those who were avid readers alike to witness a book coming to life on stage. My poetry was political, musical, radical, relevant, and, over time, on television! I was able to talk about topics that were important to me in a manner that felt true to me and people listened.

One of the areas I feel strongly about is domestic abuse. My father was very violent toward my mother. Anytime I see a frying pan on the floor I get real shivers. I remember hearing a noise downstairs in the middle of the night, and I went down and my mother and father were quiet because they were surprised that I was there, and my mother was tearful, but quietly tearful. There was a frying pan on the floor, and I thought that was a strange place for it. You don't usually see a frying pan on the floor. I said, "Mom, what is the frying pan doing on the floor?" And my mother just burst into tears and said, "Your daddy hit me with it! Your daddy hit me with it!" The first time I ever ended up in a police station it was because I stabbed my father with this little knife I had bought for sixpence, a toy really, but I had to in order to save my mother's life.

Seeing what my mother went through really made me think about women's rights. In my poetry I express my belief that in many ways women's rights have taken a step back in Britain. A lot of women think that they've arrived because they can compete with the men in the boardroom as if that's some kind of liberation. That because they can earn as much money as men, because they can drink as much beer as men and get as drunk as men, they think that's liberation. I think one has to be very careful. It's not simply just about equality. Equality on its own is not good enough. What's the use of a woman wanting equality with a man who's already oppressed? Do you want to be equally oppressed? No, we should be getting together and having full liberation. It all comes down to politics.

There's a political poem that is really crucial written by Adrian Mitchell. It's a very simple poem, only three lines and the top line is just the bottom line in a different order and the middle line is only one word. So, let me give it to you. It says:

Most people ignore most poetry
Because
Most poetry ignores most people

I think that's beautiful. And I think you can change the word poetry. You can say most people ignore most politics because most politics ignore most people. Nevertheless, positive change can happen in the most unexpected ways. I always think of the suffragette movement. Women in Britain, New Zealand, Australia, and the United States have the right to vote, and it can all be traced back to the suffragette movement. These women have gone down in history. This was never a great big, massive movement. Actually it was a small group of women who sat around eating biscuits and drinking tea, that went, "you know what, why can't we have the vote?" I want to tell people through my work to never feel that you're too small. Even if there are three of you and your cause is just, believe in it. A handful of women in London went, "Hey, we shouldn't take this," and their actions can be traced to women voting in Africa and Asia and all over the world now. It was never like the civil rights movement in the United States or anything like that. It was very small and dedicated. It wasn't about their numbers; it was the dedication they had that was important.

Resources

Adams, Barbara
Trekkies, Paramount Pictures, 1999
Trekkies 2, Paramount Pictures, 2004

Astin, Sean
There and Back Again: An Actor's Tale. New York: St. Martin's
   Press, 2004

The National Center for Family Literacy
325 West Main Street, Suite 300
Louisville, KY 40202
502-584-1133
www.famlit.org
The National Center for Family Literacy puts parents in the
forefront of their children's learning.

Bacon, Kevin
Six Degrees
www.Sixdegrees.org
Six Degrees uses the concept that everyone is separated by six
degrees to raise funds for charities.

Bardot, Brigitte

Brigitte Bardot Foundation for Animals
28 rue Vineuse
75116 Paris
France
+33 (0)1 4505 1460
www.fondationbrigittebardot.fr
The Brigitte Bardot Foundation for Animals specializes in rescuing animals, campaigning to increase spay/neuter efforts, prosecuting cruelty cases, and creating safe havens for animals around the world.

Barnard, Dr. Neal

Food for Life. New York: Three Rivers Press, 1994
Eat Right, Live Longer. New York: Three Rivers Press, 1996
Foods That Fight Pain. New York: Bantam, 1999
Dr. Neal Barnard's Program for Reversing Diabetes. Emmaus, PA: Rodale Books, 2006

Physician's Committee for Responsible Medicine
5100 Wisconsin Ave. NW
Suite 400
Washington, DC 20016-4131
202-686-2210
www.pcrm.org
Doctors and laypersons working together for compassionate and effective medical practice, research, and health promotion.

Buckley, Carol

Just for Elephants. Gardiner, Maine: Tilbury House Publishers, 2006
Travels with Tarra. Gardiner, Maine: Tilbury House Publishers, 2002

The Elephant Sanctuary
PO Box 393
Hohenwald, TN 38462
931-796-9500
www.elephants.com
A natural-habitat refuge for sick, old, and needy elephants.

Bunny, Lady

www.ladybunny.net

Coe, Sue

Sheep of Fools. Seattle: Fantagraphics Books, 2005
Bully! New York: Thunder's Mouth Press, 2004
Pit's Letter. New York: Four Wall Eight Windows, 2001
www.graphicwitness.org/coe/coebio.htm

Cohn, Susan

Jalapeño Productions
136 East 79th Street #1E
New York, NY 10021
www.runningmadness.com

The Dalai Lama

www.dalailama.com
Official Web site for His Holiness, the Dalai Lama.
Dalai Lama Foundation
61 Renato Court #24
Redwood City, CA 94061
650-368-4435

www.dalailamafoundation.org
The Dalai Lama Foundation focuses on promoting and developing projects for curriculum on ethics and peace.

Dulaine, Pierre
Dancing Classrooms
25 West 31st St.
Fourth Floor
New York, NY 10001
www.dancingclassrooms.com
Dancing Classrooms teaches ballroom dance to elementary, middle school, and high school students. Classes are available for any child regardless of background or experience.

Fernandez, Dr. Armida
Sneha, Inc.
PO Box 271650
West Hartford, CT 06127
860-658-4615
www.sneha.org
Sneha is a network for women of South Asian origin and their families that empowers women, particularly survivors of domestic violence.

Freston, Kathy
The One: Discovering the Secrets of Soul Mate Love. New York: Miramax Books, 2006
Expect a Miracle: 7 Spiritual Steps to Finding the Right Relationship. New York: St. Martin's Press, 2003
Finding a Great Relationship. (Audio CD), 2000
www.kathyfreston.com

Gannon, Sharon

Jivamukti Yoga. New York: Random House, 2002
The Art of Yoga. New York: Stewart, Tabori and Chang, 2002
Cats and Dogs Are People Too! New York: Lantern Books, 2002

Jivamukti Yoga School
841 Broadway, 2nd Floor
New York, NY 10003
212-353-0214
www.jivamuktiyoga.com
The Jivamukti Yoga Centers are places for spiritual gathering
that offer vigorous Hatha Yoga classes with an emphasis on
the source teachings from such ancient texts as the Yoga Sutras
of Patanjali and the Upanishads.

Gardner, John

ViewPlus
1853 SW Airport Ave.
Corvallis, OR 97333
541-754-4002
www.viewplus.com
ViewPlus develops technologies that minimize the communication gap between those who are blind and those who can
see. Such products include: a line of four Tiger® Braille print-
ers of various speeds and sizes, two HP Inkjet ink and Braille
systems, the IVEO Tactile-Audio System, the Tiger Software
Suite (Braille translation software and tactile graphics design
studio), as well as the Audio Graphing Calculator.

Granatelli, Andy

Scientifically Treated Petroleum (STP)
www.stp.com

Oil, gas, and fuel treatments for automobiles, STP became
famous through the racing industry.

Grandin, Dr. Temple

*Animals in Translation: Using the Mysteries of Autism to Decode
Animal Behavior.* New York: Scribner, 2005

Livestock Handling and Transport. New York: CABI Publishing,
2000

Genetics and the Behavior of Domestic Animals. St. Louis: Academic
Press, 1998

www.grandin.com

Hammarstedt, Peter

Sea Shepherd Conservation Society
PO Box 2616
Friday Harbor, WA 98250
360-370-5650
www.seashepherd.org
The Sea Shepherd Conservation Society strives to protect
and conserve marine wildlife with the goal of shutting down
illegal whaling and sealing operations.

Hartwell, Ru

Treeflights
Pantglas, Llanddewi Brefi
Tregaron, Ceredigion
Wales
SY256PE
+44 (0)15 7049 3275
www.treeflights.com
Treeflights allows airline customers to buy trees that are
planted to offset the damaging effects of their flight.

Harvey, Larry
Burning Man
415-TO-FLAME
www.burningman.com
Burning Man is a weeklong event in a temporary community
that challenges its attendants to express themselves and rely on
themselves in the Black Rock City Desert.

Heimlich, Dr. Henry
Heimlich Institute
Deaconess Foundation
311 Straight St.
Cincinnati, OH 45219
513-559-2100
www.heimlichinstitute.org
The Institute encourages others to use the creative portion of
their minds in medicine and life.

Hork, Dana
Change for Change
345 E. 77th St., Suite 2E
New York, NY 10021
www.changeforchange.org
Change for Change provides cups and other accessories to
communities that enable them to collect change to donate to
a charity of their choice.

Hosking, Rebecca

Planet Ark Foundation
Level 2, 15-17 Young Street
Sydney NSW 2000
Australia
+61 (0)2 8484 7200
www.planetark.com
Planet Ark works to help people reduce the day-to-day
impact on the environment.

Kevan, Robin

Rob the Rubbish
Llanwrtyd Wells, Powys
Wales
www.robtherubbish.com
Personal Web site dedicated to Robin Kevan's work to keep
his community clean.

Kucinich, Representative Dennis

Peace Alliance
1730 Rhode Island Ave. NW
Suite 712
Washington, DC 20036
www.thepeacealliance.org
Peace Alliance is a citizen action organization for peace.

Kuhn, Heidi

Roots of Peace
1299 Fourth St., Suite 200
San Rafael, CA 94901
1-888-ROOTS-31
www.rootsofpeace.org
Roots of Peace is dedicated to eliminating landmines and
healing the land.

Kurzweil, Raymond

The Singularity Is Near: When Humans Transcend Biology. New York: Penguin, 2006
The Age of Spiritual Machines: When Computers Exceed Human Intelligence. New York: Penguin, 2000
www.kurzweilai.net

Laflin, Bonnie-Jill

www.bonnie-jill.com
View Bonnie-Jill Laflin's acting, modeling, and sports broadcasting career.

Maathai, Wangari

Green Belt Movement
www.greenbeltmovement.org
Green Belt Movement provides income and sustenance to millions of people in Kenya through the planting of trees. It also conducts educational campaigns to raise awareness about women's rights, civic empowerment, and the environment throughout Kenya and Africa.

Mazahery, Lily

One Million Signatures Campaign
www.weforchange.info
The One Million Signatures Campaign offers support toward Iranian women who are striving to reform laws and achieve equal status in Iran.

McCartney, Sir Paul

www.paulmccartney.com

McCartney, Stella
Stella McCartney Designs
www.stellamccartney.com

McGowan, Mark
+44 (0)79 4453 3010
www.markmcgowan.org

McHenry, Keith
Food Not Bombs
PO Box 424
Arroyo Seco, NM 87514
505-776-3880
www.foodnotbombs.net
Food Not Bombs protests war and poverty while sharing free vegetarian food with the hungry.

McLaughlin, John
www.johnmclaughlin.com

Mintz, Arthur
Medical Ambassadors (now called LifeWind)
PO Box 576645
Modesto, CA 95357-6645
209-524-0600
www.lifewind.org
LifeWind works in rural villages and urban slums to empower local leaders to address their community's problems by looking at the root of poverty and disease.

Moby
www.moby.com

Mullins, Aimee
Ossur
27412 Aliso Viejo Pkwy
Aliso Viejo, CA 92656
800-233-6263
www.ossur.com
Ossur provides the most up-to-date braces, supports, and prosthetics, including Van Phillips's Flex-Foot Cheetah.

Navratilova, Martina
www.martinanavratilova.com

Nelson, Willie
Farm Aid
11 Ward Street, Suite 200
Somerville, MA 02143
800-FARM-AID
www.farmaid.org
Farm Aid raises awareness about the loss of family farms as well as raises funds to help families keep their lands.

BioWillie
Earth Biofuels, Inc.
3001 Knox Street, Suite 303
Dallas, TX 75205
866-765-4940
www.biowillieusa.com

Nemcova, Petra

Happy Hearts Foundation
131 Varick Street, Suite 921
New York, NY 10013
212-627-3220
www.happyheartsfund.org
The Happy Hearts Foundation aids children around the
world who have suffered hardship as a result of natural,
economic, and health-related disasters.

Rathke, Wade

Association of Community Organizations for Reform Now
739 8th St. SE
Washington, DC 20003
1-877-55ACORN
www.acorn.org
ACORN is the largest community organization of low- and
moderate-income families working together for social justice.

Richards, Doris

Dog Fun Directory
www.ecoanimal.com/dogfun
Offers a directory of dog parks in the United States and Canada.

Rosenthal, Rachel

Rachel Rosenthal Company
www.rachelrosenthal.org

Seegar, Dave

The Soupie at the Margaret River Community Resource Center
33 Tunbridge St.
Margaret River 6285   Australia
www.margaret-river-online.com.au/comnews/comcentre.htm

Shankar, Ravi
The Ravi Shankar Foundation
132 N. El Camino Real, Suite #316
Encinitas, CA 92024
www.ravishankar.org
Dedicated to collecting, documenting, and archiving Ravi
Shankar's work.

Sharpton, Reverend Al
National Action Network
106 W. 145th Street
Harlem, NY 10039
212-690-3070
www.nationalactionnetwork.net
National Action Network revolves around activism against
racial profiling, police brutality, women's issues, economic
reform, public education, international affairs including
abolishing slavery in Africa, job awareness, AIDS awareness,
and more.

Simmons, Russell
Russell Simmons Presents Def Poetry
www.hbo.com/defpoetry/index.html
Phat Farm
80 Enterprise Avenue South
Secaucus, NJ 07094
1-866-547-5319
www.phatfarm.com
Russell Simmons's clothing line for men and youth.

Smith, Anita
Bansang Hospital Appeal
4 The Leys
Orlingbury, Kettering
Northants NN14 1JE
www.bansanghospitalappeal.com

Stone, Oliver
Midnight Express. Casablanca Filmworks, 1978
Born on the Fourth of July. Ixtlan Corporation, 1989
A Child's Night Dream. New York: St. Martin's Press, 1997
Alexander. Warner Bros. Pictures, 2004
World Trade Center. Paramount Pictures, 2006
www.oscarworld.net/ostone

Thomas, Helen
c/o Hearst Newspapers
1850 K St. NW
Washington, DC 20006
202-263-6400
www.hearstcorp.com

Ward-Kaiser, Cheryl
The Justice and Reconciliation Project
P.O. Box 2051
Loomis, CA 95650
530-368-2026
www.thejrp.org
The Justice and Reconciliation Project is dedicated to healing
crime victims and offenders, and to communities torn by
crime.

Young, Robert
Red Feather Development Group
PO Box 907
Bozeman, MT 59771-0907
406-585-7188
www.redfeather.org
Red Feather Development Group helps American Indian families and communities to maintain sustainable housing structures and foster cultural sensitivity.

Zephaniah, Benjamin
Naked (Audio CD). One Little Indian Us, 2006
Gangsta Rap. London: Bloomsbury Publishing PLC, 2004
Face. New York: Bloomsbury USA, 2004
Too Black, Too Strong. Northumberland, United Kingdom: Bloodaxe Books, 2002
www.benjaminzephaniah.com